To my friends, Richard & Elizabeth. You are shining examples of GOD's light. Thanks for walking with Mom, me & our family on this path.

With love,

Kathy

PRAISE FOR WALKING MY MOMMA HOME

"There are truly no words for how deeply this book resonated with me. There were so many days while reading it that the bravery and authenticity Kathy showed by sharing her journey helped me face the walk I'm currently on with my parents. I laughed. I cried. And then I cried some more, but I cried tears of comfort and understanding. This book is the ultimate story of the cycle of life – the journey home – that each of us is on, and it's full of light, love and laughter along with all the tears. Thank you, Kathy, for writing such a powerful, heartfelt book and for sharing your journey and your mom's journey with the world. I'm forever grateful."

D. D. Scott
International Bestselling Author

WALKING MY MOMMA HOME

Finding Love, Grace, and Acceptance Through the Labyrinth of Dementia

By

Kathy Flora

First Electronic Edition: October 2018
First Print Edition: October 2018

eBook design & formatting by
D. D. Scott's LetLoveGlow Author Services

Dedication

To my beloved mom, Marcie,
to my dear husband, Jim, and
to my family and friends who
give me light and love, filling
me with hope for our future
and joy every day.
And, to those of you who
walk dementia's labyrinth,
may God grant to you the
same gift of love, grace, and
acceptance
that He offered me.

TABLE OF CONTENTS

Dear Reader,

This is my journey...with my soul laid bare.

While caring for my precious mom through the labyrinth of dementia, my heart has been torn open, all the junk swept out, leaving me with a life-changing affirmation.

Our lives are precious beyond anything we may ever know. Our spirits are deeper, wider and more connected than we recognize in the rush to figure out our day-to-day existence. For me, taking care of my mom slowed me down enough to see through the whirlwind of never-ending To-Do list, showing me what really mattered.

It opened a veil that had obscured my path toward heaven, and what poured out, what washed over me and into my heart was grace. Grace stretched me. It challenged me. It stripped me of things that no longer mattered. It drew me inward and upward on my path from daughter, to caregiver, to soul partner, then finally to a place of acceptance and release. Yes, it was about releasing Mom to my siblings (who also love her) and to her Creator; but for me, it was also a journey of releasing my own spirit, welcoming in more trust, more hope and the certainty that all of life (even the hardest parts) has meaning, allowing me to grow into my fullest, truest self.

Because of this journey, I am different now. My soul practically sings as I write this, for without the path I walked with Mom I may never have learned these things. Without it, I may never have been filled with the love, the hope and the joy I now carry in my heart. That is the gift that Mom gave me through the privilege of caring for her.

And it's my wish for you as you, too, embark on your caregiver's journey.

With Love and Reverence for Your Own Caregiver's Path,

Kathy

And so, it begins...

"Kathy, do you see those pink trees? Don't run into them. WATCH
OUT! Can't you see them? They're in the middle of the road.
WATCH OUT! Oh, look at those colorful ties. I wonder why they
are floating there? Do you think Jim would like one?"

With my 90-year-old mom's startling hallucinations, an
unexpected phase of life unfolded...for both of us...

Our day had started with a joyful errand, shopping for her dress
for our son's wedding, just the two of us out on a warm, sunny June
day, strolling through our local department store, eyes out for the
perfect ensemble for a beach wedding at the end of the summer. It
ended with:

- visions of pink trees in the road,
- of dogs' heads materializing through non-existent
  wallpaper,
- lines of soldiers gazing at a general who was issuing
  motivating orders on the eve of war
- and a malevolent flying squirrel whooshing by her bed in
  the dark.

These images terrorized my legally blind mom as she cowered on
top of the covers in our guest room, too frightened to sleep that
night.

What came next in my mom's descent into dementia was a
stunning, troubling, more than occasionally comical but ultimately
humbling journey of the soul. It affected each of my family members
uniquely, opening us, if reluctantly, to a world of the unknown.

For Mom, it was a serious and seemingly impossible fight as
she struggled mightily to grasp at and maintain her sense of control
despite intermittent but ever-increasing confusion.

For me and my family, it stretched us, built up walls then broke
down the barriers between us. It brought me, her primary care
partner, to my knees as I encountered one unexpected and absurd
development after another – doing my best to keep my own balance
while coping with and caring for Mom in her new, topsy-turvy

reality. Finally, it taught me, and is still teaching me, to release control, to rest, to love and to cherish small moments.

The caregiving path is a rocky one, fraught with detours, difficult decisions and spiritual challenges. It is one that so many of us will face. It's a path we travel that most surely is not the one we would have chosen for our loved one or for ourselves. Yet, how we choose to travel this road can open our eyes to a gentleness in life – a slower, more mindful appreciation of what matters when all else is stripped away.

I've discovered that I walk in parallel with Mom as her identity slowly unravels.

She is on a path facing unfathomable loss – loss of familiarity, of recognition of things present, indeed of the self that served her well for her 90+ years; yet, what she loses in her grip on reality, she is gaining in sweetness, innocence and a level of trust she could never quite grasp while wholly in control of her faculties.

The other path, mine, in this case, finds me walking this mind-altering labyrinth day-by-day hoping to grow more deeply into the higher self that God intended for me – striving to meet each new challenge with humor, grace and trust – qualities opposite my own intense, and alright, I'll say it, anxious personality, qualities I've often found in short supply in my past.

Through caring for Mom, God has given me an enormous lesson in humility and an unexpected, though often resisted, opportunity to grow into someone different in my second stage of life. My hope is that by recounting my own stumbles and stretches, our family challenges and resolutions, and Mom's fight for independence, clarity of mind and finally trust and rest, that you who are on similar paths may gain solace in the work you shoulder.

If you are caring for a loved one with dementia you certainly are not alone. According to statistics from the Alzheimer's Association, 1 in 10 people over the age of 65 in the U.S. are living with dementia. 70 – 80% of those (5.5 million people of all ages in the US) are afflicted with Alzheimer's dementia, the most common form. This number is expected to double by 2050 to 13.8 million people. Add to these numbers the more than 100 other forms of dementia, including

Dementia with Lewy Bodies (LBD - which we suspect is Mom's type and the second most common form) vascular dementia from strokes, and dementia from Parkinson's Disease, the crisis threatens to overwhelm us.

These figures are daunting. They cry out for intervention. No, they scream for a cure. And many hopeful signs for diagnosis and treatment are in the offing. But…if you are one of the many caring for someone you love who is experiencing dementia, these figures mean only one thing. You and your loved one will travel a path like none you've ever imagined. You are facing a walk into the complete unknown.

In this book you won't find medical advice for your journey. What you will find is a recounting of real-life events, emotional, humorous, poignant and infuriating events that make up the last few years I spent with my mom. I offer this story from my care partner perspective and share what I know now that you may find useful.

Let's walk together and help each other along the way.

But I'm getting way ahead of myself. Let's go back to the beginning…

Part I: Inklings of Things to Come

Chapter One:
Love and Loss

D ad died in the summer of 2004. It was an unexpected, quick, though not very merciful death. I went to visit him and my mom Marcie in their home in The Villages on his birthday, June 16th. He spent the morning making himself strawberry shortcake rather than a traditional birthday cake like Mom used to bake.

When I arrived for his birthday visit right after lunch, we enjoyed the summertime shortcake treat on the lanai. He was proud of that lanai, newly enclosed by the latest Villages' fad – removable plexiglass windows – a shield to keep out the wash of Florida's torrential summer rains. He was proud of their retirement home which they'd settled into just months before, and he was equally proud of his newly developed culinary skills.

As we savored the results of his emerging talent, we talked, we laughed, and he groused about the poor showing he had made on the golf course with his buddies the day before. We even touched briefly on my own recent recovery from cancer treatment and the entrepreneurial projects my husband Jim and I were planning now that my health storm was over.

Just before I left for the two-and-a-half-hour drive back to our home in Lakewood Ranch, I secured his commitment to look over our proposal for a new business venture, promising to send it along in an e-mail before Father's Day. Then I climbed into my car and honked goodbye: *Honk, Honk, Honk*...our family shorthand...three beeps for "I love you!"

In my mind's eye, I still see him standing in the open garage door, smiling and waving, saying, "Good Bye! Thanks for coming."

That was Wednesday afternoon. By the following Sunday, Father's Day evening, he was hospitalized with a diagnosis of pancreatitis. By Thursday he was gone. He was only 79. He had been married to Mom for 52 years and was dead two days before her own 79th birthday.

During those days of stark loss, I never saw my mother cry. A nurse until age 73, her characteristic need for control masked her pain and the threat she must have felt anticipating living alone with waning eyesight.

The only sign of uncertainty evident to Jim and me was her indecision about where to bury Dad's ashes. After his cremation, we perched his urn on the bookshelf in the living room of our rented condo for a few weeks because it scared her to keep "him" in her house. Eventually, we drove him around – the urn, I mean – wrapped in a beach towel, secured with a seatbelt in a laundry basket on our back seat, while mom checked out one cemetery after another. Ultimately she settled on one in St. Petersburg, Florida, quite a distance from her home and ours, simply because his mother and father were buried there decades and decades before. "I don't want him to be alone," she said. *Okay, Mom.* Finally, I thought. *St. Pete it is.*

The Independence Illusion

Though Mom and Dad's union was sometimes rockier than most, due to personal issues and a series of bad financial decisions that almost left them bankrupt, they seized on a fresh start in The Villages, settling into a rhythm in their retirement home including budding friendships and an unbelievable array of activities to choose from.

Mom took advantage of their new lifestyle to take low-vision classes at the Center for Sight to help her cope with macular degeneration. In those classes she learned to fold money a certain way so she could identify the denomination by the folded pattern. They taught her to use a white cane when traveling so that she qualified for extra assistance at airports, and they encouraged her to purchase and use what she called her reading machine, a specialized piece of equipment that magnified the written word up to 25X - a $2,900 prized possession. They taught her to use her finger inside a coffee cup to keep her from overflowing the cup when pouring and to put Velcro-hooked dots on her washing machine and stove, so she could feel for the settings rather than guess.

She was proud of these innovations and took to the classes like the intelligent RN that she had been.

Her instructors also informed her of a Florida state law which enabled those with vision problems to ask for shopping assistance in the grocery store when picking out items from the shelves. She simply needed to declare "I'm visually impaired," and any retail establishment would assign a helper to assist with her shopping.

This worked well most of the time, except when she was too rushed or too reluctant to ask for help. I once found three packages of small toy rocket engines rather than AAA batteries (same size, same shape) stored with the other batteries in her refrigerator crisper drawer – a practice she adopted long ago to help batteries keep their charge longer in Florida's humid air.

How do you even find rocket engines in a grocery store? No matter.

Looking back, the series of low-vision classes was one of the most important steps she took to secure her independence, not knowing at the time how crucial these tips for navigating the world would soon be.

But...rocket engines? Did they portend something more challenging than her loss of sight?

After Dad's death, each family member settled back into regular day-to-day rhythms, trusting that Mom, always fiercely resourceful and in charge, could figure out her own new rhythms for herself.

Events of the next years are a blur to me, fogged over in my mind by our move to Washington D.C., by Jim and I adjusting to a city lifestyle and my own adaptation from a budding entrepreneur to a Federal employee. We left Mom in Florida to fend for herself with the help of neighbors and close friends. During this time Jim and I weathered an occasional "Mom Crisis" causing us to make quick visits to Florida to recalibrate her finances and spending habits. "Mom, do you really need to take that cruise…give $100 to every niece and nephew at Christmas…fly to Detroit for your nursing school's May Breakfast Reunion?"

As we arranged and rearranged her household support, again and again, our trips to The Villages became more and more frequent. On one especially difficult trip we challenged her ability to drive. Ultimately when she failed to qualify to renew her driver's license, we had to sell her car.

No surprise there. Despite Florida's liberal licensing system, giving even the frailest elderly driver a 10-year renewal license if he or she could pass the written test, Mom couldn't even read the test document. Her eyesight had deteriorated so much she could no longer read magnified words on a computer screen. Her vision was 20X400 in both eyes – legally blind by anyone's standards. Her physician declined to be cajoled into giving her a written note claiming she could see well enough to drive. So, with Jim's expert persuasive skills and the doctor's support, Mom reluctantly gave up her car.

She really hated getting rid of that car and the independence it represented. Our normally safety-conscious mom was unable to accept that driving her car was a danger to both her and others. This step, more than any of the traumas of widowhood, unmasked her building resentment of Dad. "Why did he leave me in this state, and where did all my money go? I worked hard for that money and look at me now."

For months on end, every conversation centered on these two issues: Dad's disloyalty for leaving her alone and her dwindling finances. No matter how we tried to redirect the subject, her mind cycled endlessly through the same questions and resentments…over and over...and over... like an old, scratchy 45 record with the needle stuck in an endless groove, unable to move on to the next tune.

Even though it was no longer wise to maintain her free-wheeling habits, she could not seem to restrain her spending. Dad had held high-level positions in banking for much of their later married life, so she was used to virtually limitless spending on whatever she wanted. As his life came to a close, however, Dad was no longer able to make good decisions, throwing them into a dire financial crisis that took many months and major help from our entire family to unravel. Now, money was a brand new sore spot, but Mom continued spending far more than her financial status warranted.

Were this negativity and obsessive thinking just another manifestation of her personality, or was it an indication of things to come?

To address the drumbeat of almost daily negative phone calls, my older sister Lynn and I attempted to compensate for Mom's feeling of being housebound by hiring an occasional driver for her – a cheerful, middle-aged woman, aptly named Cherry. Cherry lived in The Villages, too, and supplemented her retirement income helping the older residents of the community. We found her ad in the local weekly newspaper.

In addition to driving Mom to appointments and to the grocery or Walmart once a week, Cherry cooked with Mom. Together, they would make several meals, freezing them so Mom could thaw them in the microwave or, God forbid, on the stove. The thing was, though, Mom rarely, if ever, thawed them out. Instead, I noticed a growing stack of Tupperware containers in the garage freezer, full of untouched nutritious casseroles and meat and vegetable dishes, while Mom opted for a big bowl of chocolate ice cream to satisfy her hunger and ever-present sweet tooth.

Despite the noticeable quirks, Mom's interactions with those of us in her family and in her circle of friends didn't yet raise alarm bells. I saw these issues as more of an inconvenience than as patterns of behavior that should have called all of us up short.

Driving Ms. Marcie

Eventually, in response to Mom's insistence that Cherry's 10 hours per week still left her stranded much of the time, I made a quick summertime visit back to Florida to help her map out golf cart navigation routes to the grocery, drug store and bank. That way, she could get to where she wanted to go when the fancy struck without relying on someone else. She could just hop in her cart and go.

The Villages is designed for golf carts, and it wasn't unusual to see seniors tootling up and down the cart paths in lieu of driving their cars on the roadways. If this strategy worked to help her retain her independence, Mom would be in good company.

And it was a big IF. Close your eyes and picture this...

Imagine teaching an obstinate teenager to drive in rush hour freeway traffic, in this case, though, your teenager is your 80+-year-old Mom. She's blind (okay...she says she's just "visually-impaired"...). And she insists she can see quite a bit and that she knows how to drive.

You're both perched in a golf cart, careening past other cart drivers down the wide, thankfully accommodating, cart paths for which The Villages is famous. You come to a fork in the path, and your student driver accelerates, taking you straight into the grassy median. Backing up is a challenge, but with a bit of coaching, she's able to get back on course.

But wait...what's that ahead? It's a tunnel under the busiest thoroughfare – an essential element to traverse if Mom is to safely arrive at any of her desired destinations. Looking around, you see several other carts strung out in a line behind you, heading to town in the same direction. Their drivers are getting impatient, bunching up on the curves and jockeying to pass each other before the obstacle ahead.

Yet, there it looms, the tunnel – a pitch black hole compared to the blazing glare of the summer sun – a terrible combination for a visually-impaired person. To Mom, it looks like driving into a pitch-black abyss.

Whoa! Dead stop!

The other carts screech to a sudden halt behind us, narrowly avoiding a rear-ender.

"I can't see a thing in this dark, Kathy. You'll have to take over 'til we get through," Mom said and abandoned the driver's seat... right in the middle of the tunnel.

We did make it safely home that afternoon. And in an obviously questionable move, I signed off that night on Mom's plan to use the golf cart to get wherever she needed to go – not that my permission or lack thereof would have made any difference to her.

What was I thinking as I made my way back to my life in D.C.? God only knows. But the alternative of standing up to this powerhouse of a tiny woman, who always knew her own mind and let it be known in no uncertain terms that it didn't really matter what I thought, seemed a leap way too big for me at the time.

Looking back, "denial is not just a river in Egypt," as the old saying goes. This was the state of mind that all of us "kids" lived in during those years. *Mom was doing well, right?* She knew how to manage. Everything she needed was in place – or so my siblings and Jim and I chose to believe. The truth was too overwhelming to imagine and the implications too formidable to face as each of us continued our busy lives.

Mom's Path

Although it is difficult for anyone else to understand where one's thoughts go at times of grief and massive personal change, to us, her kids, Mom's stoicism and fierce independent streak dominated the first few years after Dad died. She built strong friendships with her neighbors, kept in touch via phone and letters with old friends from our many cross-country moves and maintained her fashionable, personal style.

Although loneliness must have been a factor, she worked hard at her relationships, regularly riding to church and out to dinner with neighborhood friends. In the evenings, she could often be spotted walking the circle of the surrounding streets, gathering snippets of gossip and tossing greetings to acquaintances.

Heck, I thought, she has far more friends than I do. From my vantage point 900 miles away, she was a master at connecting with people.

After Dad died, it seemed she came into her own, forging ahead with her own plans, making independent decisions she might have deferred to Dad in the past. The occasional phone call recounting a night spent in the walk-in closet in fear of one of Florida's frequent thunderstorms, or a casual mention of a burglar who broke into a nearby home through the bathroom window were infrequent enough for us to miss her growing sense of dread and isolation. I chalked it up to Mom just being Mom.

But looking back, her medical records from this period showed her growing unease about her eyesight and her physical and neurological health. The records portray a woman seeking confirmation and answers for self-diagnosed neurological symptoms – epilepsy, a seizure disorder, heart issues, a concussion from a fall.

Although she rarely mentioned these concerns to us, she frequently consulted her neurologist and cardiologist. She refused to stop taking anti-seizure meds prescribed twenty years before despite her doctor's insistence she didn't need them. And without reporting her intent to do so to any of us, she had her neurologist conduct a test for memory, only filling us in when the results came back normal.

I can only speculate now about what she was thinking, but somehow I believe she knew what was coming…and was working her hardest to fend it off.

My Path

Do you know that old maxim "Change brings Opportunity"?

I certainly did.

I spent my professional career as a Corporate Trainer, and the Chinese symbol for *change* was a staple of the work I did with other professionals going through career transitions. Those of us in the field thought it was so slick – *Change* is written with the symbol for Danger placed over the symbol for Opportunity. We used that symbol to talk about how one could navigate the career transitions that job loss brings. We talked up change as if it were a river to cross, a road to traverse. Simply wait for the green light and over you go…if you had the right attitude.

Yeah, right!

When it came to me and Mom, maybe it would have been easier for me to grasp the magnitude of the changes we were headed for if I had taken that symbol to heart, if I had applied the wisdom behind it to my own life, wisdom I so willingly and convincingly shared with my clients.

Opportunity – for personal growth and understanding, for patience, for closer observation of the patterns I saw developing and for deeper love and respect.

Danger – for the fear of the unknown, the uncharted waters of dementia and the helpless feeling of inevitability that comes with the diagnosis.

But no, I had absolutely no idea what was to come. We didn't even have a diagnosis of the onset of dementia. I hadn't thought of Mom as old, or feeble or incapable. Heck, she had just beat me at a game of golf on The Villages course. Amazing, yes, but possible, as long as I helped line her up with the hole.

She was game for anything. She was always strong, always resourceful, always "an RN" or so she liked to tell us when she talked about the latest developments for Macular Degeneration, or seizure disorders, something she claimed to have after experiencing a seizure twenty years before at my nephew's grade school graduation celebration.

No, we had no dementia diagnosis. I had only an inkling that it would be more helpful to Mom if I visited more often, if I made an effort to call more frequently and if I helped her with her banking and personal paperwork, taxes and such, because her eyesight was a hindrance to doing these things herself.

I didn't see these things as warning signs. I just thought it all a bit inconvenient, especially since I was reestablishing myself at work in my new job in a new location.

Boy, when I look back, perhaps I was the one who was blind.

Chapter Two:
Good Friends, Gratitude and a Message from Strangers

The new year (2010) brought Jim and me back to our home in Sarasota, along with our son Dave, a rebounding twenty-something. Homesick for the light, the warmth and the beach, I secured a transfer from my job in D.C. to another federal agency with an outpost in Tampa, an hour-long commute from our home. The adjustment to my new job at age 58 was more than challenging, as was Jim's weekday travel to his job in Ohio.

There were also a lot of unexpected dynamics stirring in our lives that year, but that is a story for another time. Let's just say that one of the biggest positives from the move back to our home in Florida was being closer to Mom again.

Dealing with Mom and her frequent calls of frustration made me glad we were at least living in the same state. But we really had no idea how much her situation had deteriorated since we left Florida three years before. Most of our day-to-day interactions were still conducted over the phone except when worry, guilt or necessity prompted me to drive two hours north up I-75 after work for an overnight check-in.

After I arrived, as we'd chit-chat about inconsequential things, I could count on hearing many versions of the same story – as if her recounting them and me hearing them often enough made them true for both of us.

Covering Up the Obvious – A Newly Developing Skill

"My friends, Clarence and Cheryl, and Anne are really good to me. They watch out for me and drive me to church every Sunday. I am sure it is no trouble because they are going there anyway. I know I can call on them if I need anything."

"Leanne, my neighbor across the yard, let me stay at her house during that storm last night. Besides, I have that weather radio Lynn and Lowen bought me. I can just take it into the closet with my pillow and wait for the "all clear" if there are tornado warnings."

No matter that we are far more apt to experience the tail-end of a hurricane blow than the destructive power of a tornado in our part of the peninsula...But I digress...

"I just take the golf cart to the grocery store when I need something. It's right up the road, you know."

"There was a burglary in the next neighborhood over. Someone came in through the bathroom window. I nailed mine shut so no one could get in. Besides, I have this alarm button you set up. I'll just push it if I hear anything that scares me."

"I've got plenty to eat. Cherry cooks for me every time she comes, and she helps me out with the cleaning, too."

Why did it take so many of these comments for me to read Mom's barely-veiled anxiety and the increasingly heavy burden placed on her friends expressed by these rote tales? Why were there so many frozen dinners in Tupperware containers stacked up in her freezer? What is this sticky brown stuff all over the kitchen floor? Why has she stopped going for her 3-mile walks each night, instead retreating to the loveseat in her great room as evening comes, but not before circling every room, securing the locks and ensuring the blinds are tightly closed against a night she felt was upon her but could no longer see?

The Guilt and Gratitude Party

As our first, then our second summer back turned once again to fall and the holidays, I stewed. Nagging doubts about Mom's dependence on her friends were growing in the back of my mind.

Is it OK that Mom leans on her neighbors so much? Should I do more? How could I possibly do more? What should I do? Maybe it's OK that she depends on her friends, but certainly, we need to acknowledge their contributions. How can we thank everyone for all they do for her?

I did not like feeling beholden to anyone, even if it they were Mom's closest friends. Whenever I thought of my unexpressed gratitude, my stomach clenched in anxiety and guilt. I squirmed under the heavy weight, a burden I needed to release. Then it dawned on me. With one grand gesture, we could thank them all. That should reset the growing relationship imbalance.

"Hey, Jim, Mom has such great neighbors," I said to my husband one night after dinner, unable to stomach the worry anymore without taking some sort of action. "We had better do something to thank them for being there for her all this time. Let's cook a big Thanksgiving dinner at Mom's house this year and invite everyone who helps her out to join us for the feast."

Jim jumped on board immediately. (His loving support these past years and the steady guidance he regularly offered Mom cannot be underestimated, and he came through once again.) He switched his vacation schedule to add the Wednesday before and the Friday after Thanksgiving. We had a plan.

Email-crafted invitations went out to the friends who had been helping Mom so much since Dad died. Cheryl and Clarence, her two best friends who lived two doors down, and Anne, Cheryl's sister and Mom's dining buddy when the four of them ate out after church each Saturday night. These three became like family to Mom, with Clarence stopping by to open a jar, fix a blown fuse or pick up yard debris after a summer storm. Cheryl, a fellow RN, bonded with Mom over medical stories and was quick with a covered dish, a sweet dessert to share or an invitation to a Walmart or Walgreens shopping trip. And Anne, sweet Anne, always so thoughtful. In her free time, after hours from her banking job, she made Mom a large-print address and phone book, with letters on each page at least three inches high, each page of printer paper slipped into a plastic sleeve and ordered alphabetically. That book must have taken her hours and hours to create. It is one of Mom's most prized possessions.

After a trip to Costco for a turkey and all the fixings, even Christmas cacti, their pots festooned in fall-colored bows, to use as favors at each guest's place at the table, we were pleased with how our plan was unfolding. We'd thought of everything. We were all set.

Mom was delighted. She always loved to entertain; polishing up the good silver, getting out her favorite china and setting the table with the fine linens she kept in dry-cleaner bags in the guest room closet, in case the need to throw an elegant party arose.

As the hour for the guests to arrive drew near, I made a pass to check that the bathrooms would meet guest inspection. Mom busied herself in the kitchen peeling potatoes for Jim's famous "special mashed toes" while Jim made one final run to Publix to pick up a few more bottles of wine.

At the last minute, we learned of two additional guests, Cheryl and Anne's two brothers from Kansas just moved in to a house around the corner. Would it be okay if they joined us, they asked? Of course! What were two more when celebrating friends…as long as the wine held out, right? Thus, Jim's Publix run.

I consolidated the place settings, one more on each side of the dining table, then lit some candles in the great room, filling the room with a festive glow.

A quick knock on the door and in tumbled our guests of honor, joyfully hailing holiday greetings all around, familiar enough to pause only slightly before letting themselves in.

"Marcie, what a lovely table setting! And those flowers! Gorgeous!"

"How was your drive up, Jim? How do you like your new job,

Kathy?"

As for the extra wine, we need not have worried. The brothers possessed a sommelier's knowledge and appreciation for the stuff. They brought their own prized bottles which we promptly uncorked and savored.

What is that saying? "Serve the finest wine first."

Turkey, Potato Skins and The Brothers Speak

Well, so much for the shiny veneer of the party...behind the small talk and flickering candles, one glance over the kitchen counter revealed there was quite another story unfolding...or maybe I should say overflowing...

The home's open concept made for easy eye contact, and finally, Jim's urgent glances summoned me to where he struggled.

While I greeted guests, and Mom fawned over Cheryl's lovely outfit, Jim crouched on the kitchen floor, the sink cabinet doors open to expose the pipes. A slop of swirling, greasy, garbage water in the sink threatened to form a waterfall if he did not do something soon.

"Yech!" No plumber, Jim tried valiantly to figure out the cause of the backup, turning the garbage disposal's emergency reset by hand and flicking the on-off switch over and over. If we did not free the clog, how would we serve and then clean up after our big dinner with a torrent of garbage water cascading all over the kitchen floor?

What in the world was wrong?!

Jim and I reached the same conclusion simultaneously...

Uh-oh! Could this have anything to do with Mom's potato-peeling assistance an hour or so earlier?

Yep!

"Kathy," he whispered. "The potato skins are backing up the

sink. I can't get my hand in there to get them out, can you?"

Furtively replying that I hoped the disposal was off, I jammed my hand into the tight, gooey space to find a fibrous mash that wasn't going anywhere. The skins must have been all globbed up in the plumbing elbow, making escape for the rest of the goop in there impossible.

As we kids were growing up Mom constantly preached at us to "Never, never, never put potato or carrot skins in the disposal. They don't grind up easily and can cause a huge mess."

Well, Mom, your constant admonitions were right! How could you forget your own fundamental Marcie Kitchen Principle?!

I was fuming!

No time to worry about that now, though, I thought. Dinner was almost ready.

"Get a bucket, Jim," I whispered. "Quick!"

He snuck into the laundry room and was back in a flash with the top to the turkey roaster. "It's all I could find. It will have to do."

As Jim positioned our makeshift bucket under the sink and gingerly opened the elbow joint between the drain and the disposal to scoop out the clog, I fished slimy skins out of the opening in the sink. "Bleh!"

We finally got it cleared. One more twist of the reset key and we were in business again. Water once more flowed smoothly through the drain and pipes. The sink was operable again.

"No more potato skins in the disposal. OK, Mom?" I sent the request to her telepathically, then out loud I asked, "Mom, will you tell everyone we'll sit down for dinner in a few minutes? And how about you serve them some more wine?"

In the growing twilight, we sat around the dining table, illuminated in a soft candle glow; warm, familiar friends enjoying food, wine and the lively conversation of our newest guests "The Brothers" as Jim and I called them.

Mom sparkled, in full entertainment mode. Jim and I toasted to good friends and offered our heartfelt thanks for the assistance they had offered to our family throughout the years.

"Time for pie, everyone!"

What's Thanksgiving dinner without the pie? Conversation flowing freely, Jim cleared the plates, and I pulled pecan and pumpkin pies out of the oven. "Who wants what?"

As I turned from calling for orders over the kitchen counter into the adjacent dining room, there they were – The Brothers had joined us in the kitchen. And they had a distinct purpose on their minds.

"Kathy," one of them started, "Your mom can't live alone anymore."

There it was…the elephant in the room we had been avoiding for months…

It wasn't that we didn't see the changes in Mom's ability to cope alone, even with Cherry's help. Jim had mentioned this to me many times, warning me that I'd better talk with my sisters and brother about our next steps. I saw signs, too, but I didn't know what to do about all the little clues I observed – the frozen dinners not eaten, the chocolate ice cream smears on the kitchen floor, the dirt and dust unseen, the mold in the shower and buildup of old toothpaste drips crusted over in the bathroom sink. When we were growing up, Mom had not been a fastidious housekeeper by any means, but a clean floor and a clean bathroom were the rule, not the exception.

She covered all this so well!

Mom always looked great when we visited, stylish as ever in her fashionable clothes. Her hair was always done. When we called, she chatted amiably, sharing stories about the neighbors and all the activities they enjoyed together.

I didn't even know where to begin talking with her about the things that contradicted her carefully-crafted image of wellbeing. No, I just played along with her façade, reluctant to bring up these simple things for fear of intruding where I did not belong or of raising her defenses.

Listening to The Brothers' observations, I felt frozen, unable to clearly address their blunt statement. Once we acknowledged the truth, what were we going to do about it? They saw it clearly from an outsider's perspective and had told us so in their gentle, but firm way:

> "Your mom has been depending so much on Clarence and Cheryl and Ann, that it is getting too much for them. They love your mom, but they are getting increasingly worried about her welfare. They think she needs more help than she is getting, and they just can't keep it up. We wanted to tell you because they are too kind to say anything. We hope you understand that it is for your mom's own safety that we bring this up."

That was it. No more was said that night. We passed desserts all around while music played softly in the background, and our evening of fellowship drew to a close. As the last of our guests filed out the front door, Christmas cacti in their hands, we shared smiles and hugs all-around. Out of earshot of my mom, I quietly thanked each of The Brothers for their insights and promised to talk with my family about their concerns.

Later that weekend, I called Cheryl to ask her directly about Mom's dependence on her and her husband and sister. Was Mom causing a burden that was just too much? Cheryl was gracious and replied that, no, helping Mom was a joy, not a burden. But she did say that should it ever come to that, she would tell us.

That made me feel a bit better. I did mention The Brothers' comments about Mom's living arrangements to each of my siblings throughout the following weeks, though we didn't come to a consensus about what to do about the situation.

Then, one phone call, several months later, turned The Brother's observations into an urgent imperative to act.

The Call that Changed It All

I got the call on my cell phone while commuting home from work one early February evening.

"This is Cheryl," she began. "It's hard for me to tell you this, but your mom is become a danger to herself. I just watched her turn left in front of an oncoming car in her golf cart, and I don't think she even noticed that the driver had to swerve and slam on the brakes to keep from hitting her. I know she'll be upset that I am telling you, but not only will she get hurt, she may hurt someone else if she keeps on driving that cart. Maybe it is best if she moved closer to you."

It must have been a difficult call for Cheryl to make. After all, she was Mom's best friend in The Villages. In the years since Dad died, she and her sister Anne had pretty much adopted Mom. I assured her I really appreciated her call and reminded her that her brothers had warned Jim and me about this possibility when we were together at Thanksgiving. I should have been more vigilant about the needs they'd expressed. I apologized for not making a move to set up a better situation for Mom before now.

Cheryl, ever gentle and humble about her own needs, tried her best to let me off the hook, saying that it was hard to judge when such steps are necessary. She hung up then, most likely assured that her call would preserve Mom's safety, though it may not preserve their friendship. She was right on both counts.

"Hell Hath No Fury"

The coming weekend found me on the road to The Villages again, my own purpose top of mind. I spent the drive rehearsing what I would say to Mom, struggling with different approaches to such a life-altering message, without, in the process, incriminating her friend Cheryl as the snitch.

But when I walked into the house that evening, surprising mom as she dozed on the loveseat in the great room, my heart told me, "Just state the facts outright, Kath. Mom deserves to hear the truth."

"Mom," I began, as she inquired, with alarm in her voice, about what brought me all the way up there that evening? "I heard from a friend of yours this week who is really concerned that your golf cart days are over."

"Who dared call you about me?" She drilled.

"You are lucky you have friends who love you, Mom. Cheryl called. Did you realize that, the other day when you were out in your cart, you turned in front of an oncoming car? The driver had to slam on the brakes and swerve to avoid hitting you. Cheryl said you did not even stop. She was pretty sure you were not even aware of the chaos you caused with that turn. Do you know what I am talking about?"

Rather than deny the incident, Mom retreated into an angry, defensive posture, exclaiming, "How dare she call you! I am going to go right over there and tell her to mind her own damn business! She doesn't know what she's talking about!"

Oh, boy! Did I ever stir up a hornet's nest? Somehow, I'd thought that using reason – and the knowledge of her friend's care for her in making that call – would soften the news, allowing Mom to process it rationally.

But for the rest of the evening, she refused to even talk about other ways to handle the message I brought with me. Could we get Cherry to drive her more often? What if she moved into an apartment closer to me so that I could drive her where she needed to go?

She was having none of it, storming out of the room and slamming her bedroom door for emphasis.

Defeated, for now, I headed off to the guest room, pulled down the Murphy Bed and crawled in.

I shed tears of frustration that night while stressing mightily about what I knew was the right thing to do, but what Mom also refused to see. Instead, she vowed to cut off her friendships with the people closest to her, vengefully claiming she would just have to take care of herself from now on.

"God, please," I begged in my prayers that night, "Give me the words to say that can make this better for everyone. I don't know what else to do, Lord. I just don't know what to do." I drifted off to sleep, focusing over and over on my fervent prayer. "I don't know what to do, Lord. Please show me what to do."

Early the next morning, before I ventured out of my safe-haven, Jim and I brainstormed by phone. Mom's fierce reaction was certainly in character. But I wanted no part of her biting accusations. We both wanted to be sure to preserve relationships, with Mom and among the rest of the family. Yet, her safety and the liability we carried by owning the home she lived in pressed hard on us.

Ultimately, we decided to pull no punches and to use what you might call "the nuclear option." When Mom and Dad lost their financial footing the year before they moved to Florida, we had purchased The Villages' home. They paid us nominal rent, but the power of the purse would be our ace-in-the-hole now. We decided to tell her that we were going to have to sell the house and help her move to Sarasota near us so that we could be there for her as much as she needed.

The way we saw it, what other choice did we have? She refused to recognize her own peril.

We planned to give her six weeks' notice so that we had time to make all the moving arrangements, but a short enough duration that her time alone (two hours from the help we could offer) seemed manageable.

April 1st was our deadline. Mom was 86-years-old. Although dementia was not yet an obvious element, her macular degeneration made a move to a new home a challenging prospect. It took every free moment in that six weeks to orchestrate her move, from finding an apartment in a suitable facility, to engaging Mom and my sibs in the planning and actual move.

For me, Jim and Mom, the challenges of this move were not all the obvious ones such as locating and renting a place and deciding what furniture would fit into the new space. The bigger challenges were decisions of the heart.

How do we best engage our family members? Since they live elsewhere, should we include them in all these decisions or just inform them of the outcomes of the decisions? How much could/ should I ask of them? What if they ask things of us to which we cannot agree? What do I do or say if they push back or say no to what we've decided? Is this a democracy? Whose votes count? And do anyone's opinions count more than others?

How do Jim and I adjust our lifestyle to accommodate a newly-assumed responsibility for another person?

How do I find energy and spirit to navigate a new way of talking and acting with my mom, so that her dignity and independence are preserved, yet she's protected from decisions and actions that could harm her?

And how do I take on this new role, with all its implications, while managing to juggle my intense work schedule, the remote living arrangements of my marriage at the time and the other daily issues that make up a middle-aged life?

Yes, these were important questions. Profound questions. But when faced with the first crisis of my Mom's declining health – moving – I confess, my instincts took me in an entirely different direction, focusing my energies where I knew I could succeed. After all, I had navigated many family, cross-country moves with kids, dogs, cats, and aplomb. Certainly, I could do this one. So, step back, and get out of my way!

During the initial six weeks' crunch time, I flipped into tactical mode, all organization and analysis. And so, enlisting Jim's help, we dug in to answer the practical questions: What living options in Sarasota were best? What could Mom afford? How do I get the best movers? How do we sell the house? One thing after another, on and on. It required a spreadsheet to keep it all straight.

The rest, the important soul stuff…well…that would have to wait.

Mom's Path

Can you imagine the blow it must have been for Mom to hear, "You can't live here anymore," let alone hear that the message came indirectly from your best friend, one you trusted and depended upon? Mom was reeling. I can feel her thoughts sizzling that morning as she hurled out: "Who was I to tell her that? Who was Cheryl to speak those words of betrayal...words that would alter her life forever." "How dare she speak for me!" "How dare you intrude in my life, Kathy!" And most hurtful, "You'll get yours, you kids will see. I'll spend all my money, then you'll just have to take care of me. You'll get yours!" That was the one my sister Lynn and I heard most often: "You'll get yours!"

Anger masked her fear. Anger welled up and uncovered old wounds of other betrayals in her life. Her anger rose white hot. She was seething. Making a thoughtful, constructive approach to finding solutions was impossible for her for now.

Anger also masked her feeling of defeat. She had been found out. The mask was off. All her effort to hide her growing unease and debility was undone. She was losing control of her life, of her future. This was not at all what she had planned.

Who could blame her for her anger. I would be angry, too.

My Path

This was not what I signed up for either.

But the specter of a crash – golf cart versus delivery truck or one of those big Lincoln Town Cars driven by Florida seniors – haunted me.

Of all Mom's kids, I felt like the last one who should tell her she was no longer able to live alone. I know I was the one closest in geography, but to tell you the truth, she intimidated me, and our adult friendship was fragile, still developing. We didn't have a very positive relationship throughout my teen years, and I'd worked hard in adulthood to mend the rift my own actions and attitudes created. We did get along, but I had to feel my way carefully so that old reactions and resentments didn't rear up and bite both of us.

But dang, this one was so much bigger than me. This one called on a spirit I had only recently recognized as "God in real time." Would He be there for Mom like He was for me and our immediate family when other crises loomed?

The faith from my childhood was strong, but this crisis with Mom was going to require Adult Faith, with a capital A and F. And I was on my way to discover more and more about this faith with each passing day.

Neither Mom nor I were prepared emotionally or spiritually for the walk ahead. I think that it was easier for me to live in the traditional child/parent mode (allowing Mom to make her own decisions no matter how fraught with peril) than it was to nudge my heart into an ever more necessary care partner role. If Mom portrayed the contented elder – seemingly enjoying life in one of the country's top retirement communities – I could happily ignore any signs of trouble potentially brewing.

I did not want, nor choose, to be a caregiver. I sensed that the role, as it evolved over time, would be more challenging than anything else I had encountered. It was a role I was not at all certain I could fulfill.

Chapter Three:
Heart Search…Home Search

While Jim handled the terms of the realtor arrangements from a distance, setting the selling price and listing the house in The Villages, I focused on searching for the best place for Mom in our hometown. I say, "best place for Mom", but to tell the truth, in the initial stages, I searched, then Jim searched with me, without consulting Mom.

I quickly became an expert in our local Independent Living and Continuing Care Facilities. My focus was on affordability, proximity to our house and an activity roster that would engage a new resident, so friendships could develop. With the limiting factor of affordability, however, we had to eliminate many of the continuing care communities. They were lovely places, with attractive features, but they required a buy-in upfront. Perhaps many seniors who choose these communities have a home to sell and a big pile of equity from that home that they use to pay the entry fees. But not in Mom's case.

Mom and Dad had sold their home in Seattle and a chalet in northern Michigan, taking their equity to pay off debt, leaving them with very little savings. In fact, Mom's main source of income after Dad died was a draw on the small life insurance policy he left her, a small 401(k) from her nursing years and her Social Security check. The latter was substantial, compared to many her age, since she claimed on Dad's income before their financial debacle. But still, it wasn't a lot, considering the fees required for most of the communities we found. Her reality was that we had a financial limit to manage. We tried our best to find a place to rent with all the amenities we thought she needed while keeping her monthly expenses within budget. No small feat.

I visited no fewer than seven independent living facilities, narrowing the choices down to three.

Then, one Saturday afternoon while home for the weekend, Jim drove around and looked at the three choices with me. His reaction was like Goldilocks'. One was too old. One too far from our house. One too la-dee-da and snooty.

How were we ever going to find a place for Mom?

As we headed home discouraged, we passed a sign that said, "Desoto Beach Club, Tours Daily." Jim made a quick left turn up the drive and around a bend.

Desoto Beach Club looked just perfect. It was cute, clean and close. The facility was part of a nationwide chain, with reasonable rent for a one-bedroom apartment, 3 daily meals plus snacks and a roster of weekly activities should one want to participate. It had an on-site physical therapy group, a beauty parlor, and a chapel. It even had a pool, a feature that seemed really important to me, though, I never saw anyone use it the entire time Mom lived there. The facility had just opened six months or so before our search and wasn't fully-occupied. This meant Mom could choose from several apartment locations on one of three floors.

Time to bring Mom into the picture. You think? Oh, and my older sister Lynn, too. Since she was able to come down from Indianapolis to help with the move, we lined up a few days in Sarasota for Lynn and Mom to review the choices.

Hell-bent on getting this big move done, I didn't pay much attention to the impact the time pressures put on my mother or any of my siblings. Lynn probably told me she thought we were moving too fast. And I am certain Mom did. But I cannot recall the specifics of those conversations. It was only later when another potential move loomed that we talked about the impact of rushing things.

That instinct was right on many counts. Disruption was hard on Mom. But the thing that mattered most to me was settling this move and settling it soon. Mom was not safe in The Villages, after all, her neighbors told us so. Time was wasting. Let's get this done!

We took Mom to visit the first two of our final three options in one afternoon, saving the third, and what Jim and I determined was the best choice, for the following day. Mom's head must have been reeling with all the changes she was facing, not the least of which was her sight issue. How adaptable would she be able to be in a new home, knowing her eyesight was failing? We weren't oblivious to the challenge, but still, we charged ahead.

That second afternoon, our trip to the Desoto Beach Club was a success. The kind, welcoming managers made Mom feel she would have an instant connection should she move in. They showed us several apartments, all lovely. Each was equipped with a small kitchen – sink, cupboards, no stove, but a full-sized fridge. There were three huge closets and even a small, screened lanai, an essential, we thought, for sitting on the porch in the breeze during Florida winters.

One apartment, although looking out over the parking lot, was the brightest, since it received the morning sun. It was also on the second floor, so we hoped there would be no fear of intruders coming through the windows, and it was past the fire doors. This feature seemed most important to Mom because suddenly she expressed fear of not being able to get out of the building if there was a fire. Mom chose the bright, second-floor, fire door one, Apt 235.

With everyone in agreement, we signed the lease that afternoon and planned a move-in date of mid-April. *What a relief.* This place was only fifteen minutes from our home, right by shopping and close to where a new mall was being planned. It had a shuttle to doctors' appointments and activities around town.

What more could someone ask for, right? It checked all my boxes...but what about Mom's?

What about Mom?

I'll tell you what...Mom was MAD! And I mean MAD!...for a

while...a long while.

And no wonder she was MAD!

She was mad at Dad for dying, mad at the world because she worked so hard for so long and lost so much money, mad at her friends for snitching on her and mad at her circumstances. And probably, she was especially mad at us, though I seldom heard her express it directly.

But remember, Lynn and I did catch the brunt of that anger when she proclaimed, "You kids will get yours!"

That stung, and I recall feeling self-righteous anger at her indignant outburst.

But can you blame her?

Mom raised 5 kids, each of us successful in our own way. She and Dad gave us many privileges while we were growing up. I think if I were in her shoes (and I may be someday, sooner than I may choose), I would be MAD, too.

With all these emotions swirling, mid-April came upon us with unmerciful speed. While Jim and I returned to work at our respective jobs, me in Tampa and him in Ohio, Lynn drove Mom back to The Villages to plan which of her belongings would work in the new apartment. Then, she made her way home to Indiana only to return a few weeks later to pack up or dispose of the remaining household goods once the move was done.

Confusion Reigns

Increasing blindness from macular degeneration and the resultant self-care issues it brought may have sparked the necessity for Mom's move to an independent living facility, but the beginnings of confusion, and possibly even looming dementia, reared its head as moving day approached.

As Lynn recounts, after driving Mom back up to The Villages

before she returned home to Indianapolis, Mom and she made great progress deciding what to bring to the DeSoto Beach Club and what to dispose of – whether to a charity, to sell or to give to family members. Mom trusted Lynn's judgment, and she readily agreed to give away much of her furniture, at least for now.

Before Lynn flew home, they took pictures and measured all the pieces of furniture that Mom chose to keep, working together to determine the layout and design of each of the rooms in Mom's new apartment. It would be lovely, Mom agreed.

That seemed normal, right? Well, not for long…

As moving day loomed, I took a few days off work to help Mom pack, driving up to The Villages from Tampa. I arrived around 3 PM. I thought Mom was expecting my arrival. But judge for yourself…

As I parked in the drive and got out of my car, I noticed three figures in the darkened garage standing by the open door. Mom, my Aunt Sally (mom's younger sister) and her husband, my Uncle Mike.

Aunt Sally and Uncle Mike were cherished members of our family, beloved by all. I knew them well. In my earliest memory of them, I was 4-years-old, riding joyfully along with my sisters and cousins in the back seat of Uncle Mike's convertible the day before their wedding while he took us on pre-wedding errands just to get us all out from underfoot while plans for the ceremony were in full swing at Grandma's house.

So, when I walked into the garage, I greeted them warmly. "Hi, everyone! So happy that you came."

"Oh, who is this?" Mom said and turned to me.

I assumed the light from the outside temporarily blocked her vision, but why didn't she recognize my voice?

After a lengthy pause, she said, "Oh, it's Kathy. Kathy, I want you to meet my sister, Sally and her husband, Mike."

Whoa! What just happened? Did she just introduce me to Aunt Sally and Uncle Mike? She sure did.

~36~

The three of us exchanged puzzled looks over Mom's head. This was going to be a challenging move. That much was clear.

After Sally and Mike departed, Mom and I set out to pack the remaining items in her kitchen and linen closets, readying everything for the movers to come the next morning. By midnight, everything was all set, or so I thought. But once I retired for the night, exhausted after hours and hours of packing boxes, Mom snuck back into the great room and undid all our hard work. She dug back into box after box, removing items, resorting and mixing up the contents of others, so that the labels were meaningless. She seemed particularly focused on the pillows – which pillows to take, which to get rid of, which went with her bedspread. Oh, and she just had to take her custom, king-sized bedspread and matching draperies and rods. It didn't matter that her new apartment bedroom only had room for a queen bed, and the draperies and rods, no matter how lovely, would not fit the windows in her new place.

A challenging move…oh, yeah! Challenging? Well…that was an understatement.

Mom's Path

Mom used to be a pro at moving. After all, we had moved so many times as a family when I was growing up that she had to be good at it. From Michigan, to Minnesota, to Connecticut, to Pennsylvania, back to Michigan, to Seattle, then Michigan again, then Seattle again. Who could keep up?

This move was different, though. This time she was moving without Dad, without most of her stuff and with waning eyesight and a growing awareness that something wasn't quite right neurologically,

~37~

regardless of what her doctors told her.

She masked her fears with cooperation and a stoic acceptance, except for a sharp remark or a worried expression here and there that revealed her angst.

But this had to be her hardest move yet. *How would she make friends again? Would she be able to recognize people when she saw them in the hall? Would they accept her into their circles?* Aren't these the uncertainties we all face when we encounter a new, unfamiliar situation? All of us want to belong, to be liked, to fit in. Now, at 86-years-old, she had to face it all over again.

A move takes guts. It took all she had to navigate this one.

My Path

Moving day. I remember it vividly. This was not a day for sentimentality. It was a day for looking forward. And so, Mom and I stood watch as the movers tagged and carried boxes to the waiting truck, checking off each one on the inventory sheet they provided. With one last look around and a brief salute to all this home had meant, "*Honk. Honk. Honk*", and we were off toward life's next stage.

So why does it hurt my heart to write this? Why does sadness well up and overflow my eyes as I think back on the meaning of this transition?

Because I was right there with her, experiencing a deep thread of loss, a sense of the inevitability of life's seasons passing, of uncertainty for the future. What will the next season bring?

If only we could slow down time.

"God, please make this move a good one," I prayed. "Please help Mom understand."

Part II: The Age of Independent Living

Chapter Four:
The Good Years – A New Home and New Hope

Settling In

Despite the inauspicious beginning, Mom thrived in the Desoto Beach Club.

Those first few weeks, her resourcefulness and fierce independence served her well. Within days of her move, her confusion cleared – thank goodness. She sorted out her belongings, quickly made decisions on what went where, what to leave packed up and what she needed to purchase for life to be as comfortable as possible.

We went shopping for a small microwave and a small painted cabinet to hold it. We bought new sheets, towels, and a shower curtain to lend a colorful touch to her spacious bathroom. And, we hung a welcoming flower wreath on the door to entice visitors to stop by.

Very quickly, Mom found three dining buddies, and they soon became fast friends, accompanying each other at every meal, at events, on shopping trips, and to Bingo on Wednesday evenings after dinner. Each new friend came with intriguing stories, so table conversation never lagged. Ellen, Agnes, Anne, and Marcie – they were inseparable. Things at "The Beach Club" turned out better than

Mom had imagined. Life was looking up again!

New Love

Since we were only fifteen minutes down the road, Jim and I visited often. We frequently shared meals together with Mom's Beach Club friends and soon embraced them as part of our family, too. Ellen, especially...Ellen was our favorite, and Mom's.

One of the frequent jokes between them was they had to keep their eyes out at dinner for a rich husband...for then, they would have no worries. You would have thought we were back in our college dorm cafeterias, watching all the roving eyes in the dining room. It was fun to be part of the excitement, always wondering, "Who is sweet on whom now?"

Then...came Frank. Frank was my dad's name. But this Frank was a new man entirely. Frank, from Ohio, who used to own pizza parlors. Frank, who we found out much later, founded the pizza shop that was Jim's and my favorite Friday night hangout.

Frank found Mom in the dining room, eight months after she moved in. And this Frank changed her life.

He wooed her, charmed her and made her feel like a school girl, all giggly, dreamy and smiling non-stop. Suddenly, her hair had to be perfect again, her nails had to be polished again and her clothes had to be meticulously selected for effect on her new love.

She couldn't get enough of him, and he couldn't get enough of her. They were together constantly, holding hands, snuggling on the couches, and who knows what else. I certainly didn't want to know.

But she did fret...how far should she go? Would they marry? If not, was it okay to bend the rigid rules from her strict, Catholic upbringing? Mom only mentioned that one to me once, most likely judging by my reaction that she was much better off making that decision on her own.

The romance was a turning point in confidence for Mom. It had been a long time since she felt so desirable, so beautiful, so honored for her smarts and her conversational gift.

We loved this guy. And who wouldn't? He loved Mom so intensely. We invited him to join our family gathering at our home for Thanksgiving, and he introduced us to his son and daughter-in-law, inviting all of us to their home for dessert. His son's family also seemed to love Mom. Soon, we, too, began to wonder if they would marry – even at their advanced ages, their infatuation was infectious.

Frank helped Mom set up and decorate her little Christmas tree, and they celebrated the holidays together. He bought her flowers and escorted her to the Valentine's dance at The Beach Club. And since he still had those most cherished of possessions, a car and driver's license, Frank drove Mom and her friends on errands. They spent time at the beach, went out to lunch and roamed the town in his sedan, content to explore the city or just go get an ice cream cone, as long as they were together.

A Player or A Gentleman?

Then, as quickly as it started, it was over. Frank called Mom one afternoon and left her a voicemail, stating he was no longer going to be able to see her.

The weekend before, his son had helped him move to an apartment in Sun City Center, about forty minutes north of Sarasota via I-75. Mom was aware of the move, even involved in selecting furniture for his new place. She was under the impression from their conversations about it that once Frank got settled, he would help her move in with him. In her mind, they may not get married right away, or at all, but she envisioned life together for the rest of their lives.

A voicemail?! It was today's equivalent of a text message breakup!

"What a coward!" Mom raged.

She reached out by phone, but Frank never picked up. So, she wrote him a blistering letter, calling him a cad, a playboy, and a bastard. "Every name in the book," she recounted. Then, she wrote him off.

Still, she stewed, wondering what could have precipitated his abrupt about-face regarding his feelings for her? What if a simple errand may have sparked their breakup?

A few weeks before he left the voicemail, Frank drove Mom to the License Bureau to update her state-issued ID so they could travel by plane together whenever they felt like getting out of town. Maybe Frank saw her birthdate on the written application. Maybe he found out she was five years older than he, ready to turn 88 that coming June. Maybe their age difference freaked him out.

Certainly, Mom was able to keep up with him, and with her facelifts years before, she looked much younger than her 88 years. But perhaps his rash decision to break up relieved him of an imagined future with an aged partner much less able than he was.

Or, as I prefer to believe, maybe the opposite was true and his breakup was the kindness of a gentleman, meant to spare Mom from being saddled with a partner who was facing growing infirmity.

Mom never did find out the true reason for his withdrawal from her life. But a year or so later, on a Beach Club bus trip to Publix, she ran into his daughter-in-law. She told Mom that for the past year, Frank's health had been giving him a great deal of trouble. He had to move back in with them. He had deteriorated drastically, and his heart was giving out.

We will never know for sure why Frank left Mom, and why he did so in such an awkward, impersonal way. But what I do know is that his big, loving heart jumpstarted my mom's. Sharing a brief time with her, giving her gifts of joy, laughter and love left her transformed.

More of the Good Years

The next two and a half years in the Desoto Beach Club passed with a steady rhythm of a well-ordered life. Mom maintained her friendships with her table buddies and grew especially close to Ellen, whose family was too busy raising kids and dealing with the illnesses of other family members to be as attentive to her as Mom judged they should be.

We often included Ellen in outings for ice cream any time we stopped by to take Mom out for a treat. We just loved her company. She was gracious and fun loving, teasing Jim that he promised her another ice cream date, never letting him forget she was going to hold him to that promise.

Mom and Ellen fell into a sisterly dependence, enjoying daily activities and looking out for each other. If one did not make it down for a meal, the other checked in immediately. If one was feeling ill, the other made sure a tray was delivered, ensuring nourishment to shorten whatever ailment had raised its head. That is until Ellen confessed to Mom one day that she had survived a cancer of the digestive system, and sometimes, just couldn't face coming down for dinner. Her confession, held in confidence, made Mom even more solicitous to her friend, raising both her compassion and her long-dormant RN skills.

Soon they began a nightly ritual, sitting on the veranda after supper with friends, rocking and talking until the mosquitos or the chilly breeze drove them inside. Then, Mom would walk Ellen back to her room at the end of the First-Floor corridor, the blind leading the infirm, Mom ensuring Ellen was safely ensconced in her studio apartment before taking the stairs to her own room upstairs on Two.

Just as Mom and her friends fell into an easy existence, so, Jim and I and my siblings found it easy to fall back into our daily lives, no longer worried about Mom. With regular meals and social interaction, both her health and her cognitive ability improved. She put on pounds, and her thinking improved. Visits and calls were met with tales of the fun she had with her friends or the latest gossip from The Beach Club, as well as eager questions about our lives and the lives of her many grandchildren.

Mom's family was growing, too, with four new grandchildren arriving in the ensuing two years. First Eli, then Jackson, Emmie, and Drake, all born within months of each other. Jackson was Jim's and my first grandchild, born of our youngest son David and Lindsey, right here in Bradenton. He arrived six weeks early and spent sixteen scary days in the NICU until his lungs could safely support his tiny body.

We all doted on our precious baby boy, and Mom was no exception. We often picked her up to visit us when we babysat Jack. She was so happy he lived close by, always ready to snuggle him, sing him to sleep and watch him grow. Nothing brought more joy to her face than the opportunity to hold him close to her heart and coo loving messages into his tiny ears.

This forged a bond that is as strong as life itself. As Jack grew into a toddler, a preschooler then a precocious young man, the two of them shared jokes and Hot Wheels, silly songs and birthday celebrations, chocolate kisses and Christmas surprises like a goofy, piano playing Santa, not to mention the special toys lovingly scouted out from the Dollar Store on Beach Club Shopping Tuesdays.

Just as Jack is precious to Mom, Great Grandma is precious to Jack. As she had comforted and nurtured him as a small child, he could be found as the years and infirmity took an inevitable toll on her, comforting and caring for her, sharing his beloved "Georgie" the monkey, snuggling her – pulling her blankets close when she was cold and leading her down the hall with her hand in his, opening doors for her, making sure she got to the dining room without hurting herself.

He exhibited God's grace itself, and far, far more empathy and compassion than one could expect from a young boy.

But I'm getting ahead of myself…again…

Mom's Path

At first, the move to Independent Living at The Desoto Beach Club seemed to Mom like a move to a prison, the last stop at the end of the line. But as it turned out, she thrived in her new home.

Adding the simple support of meals at regular times, with enough nutritious choices to appease her preferences, improved her physical health. And by eliminating her fear of sleeping alone in a solitary house, her sleep patterns improved. She thrived as she hadn't in the years since Dad died.

But it was love that truly made a difference in adapting to her new surroundings. The love of new friends, the true love of a gentleman destined to stay for but awhile and the love of family, especially one little guy, who gave her a renewed sense of joy and purpose.

These were, indeed, the good years.

My Path

What I had dreaded, having Mom living so close that I was the one to care for her daily needs, became one of my own biggest joys.

This was the first extended period I had lived near her, or anyone but my immediate family, since Jim and I married more than 35 years before. Jim, me, our older son Mark, David, and our cat Cotty – that was our nuclear family for all the years the boys were growing up. But as we spent time together with Mom and celebrated day-to-day life, reminiscing about the past, chatting about people and events and observing her within her own social circle, I came to know her as a woman of substance.

She had raised five of us and moved all over the country, successfully settling in each time, making friends and connecting in her newest community. At Christmas, she still maintained contact with women from the neighborhoods we lived in when I was a child. This woman knew how to build and nurture relationships. And she proved it this time, too. I could learn something from her devotion to her friends, her connection to their lives and her ability to rally to whatever situation in which she found herself.

As I observed Mom through these good years, I thought one word described her best – *Fierce*. She loved fiercely, she fought for her independence fiercely and she defended and cared for her "tribe" fiercely. I wanted her strength. I wanted to be FIERCE, too.

Chapter Five:
Pots, Pans and Financial Independence

I f the years between Mom's move at 86 and her turning 89 brought a reprieve from worry about her safety and growing blindness, the minor concerns that showed themselves in The Villages remained.

The adjustment to a more frugal lifestyle continued to be a difficult one for Mom. She was a spendthrift; she bought what she wanted, not just what she needed. And, she never saw a gadget she didn't want, especially if it held promise for improving her eyesight or her longevity. She ordered vitamins and supplements from the latest health store catalogs, doodads from TV shopping channels and bought her clothes from Dillard's and Nordstrom's when she could get there.

Mom loved beautiful things – beautiful clothes, jewelry, the latest household décor. She was used to a life surrounded by these things and didn't want to give them up. "After all," she said, "I worked hard for my money. I should be able to spend it how I want!"

I couldn't argue with her there. She had worked hard. But what she had saved from their financial downfall, her small pension from her nursing years, and Dad's life insurance policy would have to last a long, long time.

To ease her mind, Jim calculated what he considered a reasonable monthly budget and talked her through the numbers. At the spending pace he laid out for her, her funds should last until she was 93. She figured that since her own parents and their siblings lived into their late 80's and early 90's, that should be long enough.

Now, if we could only get her to live by that financial plan, she'd be all set.

When she moved to Sarasota, Jim and I helped with change of addresses on magazines and her books on tape for the blind and with updating the Social Security Administration and Medicare of her new location. We introduced her to our attorney who updated her will, her advanced directives, power of attorney and health care surrogates, just in case.

Mom was glad to have these fundamental arrangements made ahead of any potential crisis, understanding that it was better to set them up herself, so her wishes would be clear.

I also helped her establish a savings and checking account at a local bank, arranging for direct deposit of her Social Security checks. Because she could not drive nor see well enough to write her own checks and pay her bills, we arranged for my name to be on her accounts. And to alleviate some of her worries about running short, we arranged monthly auto-transfers from her small investment account to her checking account for her Beach Club rental fees, phone and other utilities, and some extra cash for daily expenses.

It felt to us like we had taken care of everything – for now.

Normal Life – Let's Celebrate!

During these good years, I found that visiting once or twice a week and keeping up with regular phone calls were all that were needed to stay in touch with Mom. I was working in Tampa and the drive to her apartment was twenty minutes further south than our new condo along the Manatee River.

We had recently downsized into condo living after selling our house and returning home from D.C. in 2012. Once we saw that

Mom had stabilized, we made the move to shorten my commute by an hour each day. Less time commuting was a welcome relief. So, too, was the sense that Jim and I could stay on top of Mom's needs and engage her in our family lives at a pace that seemed like any normal family.

We picked up Mom to come over for dinner regularly, and she celebrated all the holidays with us, Easter brunch, 4th of July fireworks, barbecues for birthdays and Christmas.

Christmas was a big affair at our house. In keeping with a long-standing family tradition, I usually went overboard, just like Mom had in our childhood. I guess that was one of the things I inherited from her. Every decoration had to be just right, yards and yards of lace wrapped around our staircase banister and the pillars in the dining room festooned with twinkling lights shining through, the Christmas Village (a gift from Mom on successive Christmases) set up high above the kitchen cabinets and the ceramic nativity scene, with the Baby Jesus missing until Christmas Eve.

Gifts were stacked waist high, and delicious food and sweet treats overflowed the counters and fridge. I thrived then and still do on setting a magical scene like the Christmases I remember from my childhood.

We established a tradition of inviting Mom to spend the night on Christmas Eve, so she could participate in dinner with friends and whatever family members weren't working that night. Best of all, she could be there in the morning to savor the excitement and warmth of family when Jack and his momma and daddy came by to open the gifts Santa left at Grandma and Grandpa's house.

Yes, it was nice having Mom around. It felt like home.

Living in the Now…Anything but Ordinary

Most Saturdays, I headed a few exits down I-75 to check in with Mom at her place. We took weekly runs for errands, stopping first at the bank for Mom's essential pocket change and Bingo cash.

We'd hit the grocery and drug store or whatever else we decided in the moment, including scouting for door decorations for her apartment to distinguish her home from the others in her hallway.

Mom had access to The Desoto Beach Club bus for regular outings and shopping trips which she took advantage of on a weekly basis, but the time that we spent together on Saturdays forged a close bond as we giggled over exciting fashion finds at Fifi's Fine Resale Apparel Shop, picked out chocolate goodies at Publix to sustain her snack-binging for the week or took a "day of beauty" getting our nails done together at a local salon.

Having Mom nearby could be a gas. I grew to truly enjoy her company.

As time went on, I found she needed more and more of my help keeping things up in her apartment, so on a weekday evening, either Jim or I would swing by to pick up her laundry to be returned on Saturday when I came by again.

Mom had a newly acquired habit of changing into two or three outfits a day, along with fresh underwear with each change, and she used a clean towel and several washcloths every day.

Was she having trouble with incontinence? I didn't think so because she frequently complained about constipation. *And weren't those conditions opposites?* She was just being fastidious about her dress and appearance, a good sign, I thought.

But it was increasingly hard for her to keep up with what to wear, thus the ever-overflowing laundry basket.

On the surface at least, it was easy to see why. Mom had tons of clothes and loved to be fashionably dressed. From the look of her closets, one would think she saved every outfit she ever owned. She had dresses from the 70's, pants from her days of Size 4, formals from our respective weddings and a fur coat or two that kept her warm and stylish in the north before the days of PETA and splashed paint. Her three closets were jammed. Sorting the wearable from the "I just can't let that go" was a challenge.

I took it on, though. I sorted her closets by season and arranged everything by color and type, untangling and disposing of hundreds of wire hangers and putting shoes and innumerable purses in boxes to make them more accessible.

Still, her eyesight made selecting things that matched or complimented each piece a challenge for her. And that was nothing compared to sorting out all her costume jewelry. She had a tall, wooden jewelry chest full of earrings, bracelets, and necklaces, from the Mardi Gras beads of last month's Beach Club party to puka shells from Hawaii and gold and silver chains, broaches and circle pins that were gifts from Dad. Oh, and of course, a red velvet bag tied with a woven silk ribbon that held all the heirloom pieces and the "real" gold she kept in an unlocked safe on the floor of her bedroom closet.

Mom took special delight in placing each piece of jewelry under her reading magnifier machine, sorting earring pairs and placing them in tiny glassine bags or in the squared off compartments the top drawers of her jewelry chest offered. It was as if with each pair or strand she reminisced, thinking about the day when she'd worn the outfit, and the earrings graced her ears. With those memories, she was vitally engaged in her world again.

On one winter weekend, when Lynn and my younger sister Peg visited from up north, the three of us tried again to streamline the closet space and jewelry to help her sort out the wearable from the museum-ready (more like black trash bag ready) pieces. From our perspective, all the extra clothes weighed her down and made her daily life messier and more confusing.

Maybe, this time, Mom would agree to the winnowing.

Mom and we sisters spent a joyful, girly afternoon rummaging through the slacks, purses, and baubles. Lynn brought plastic potato chip bag clips to link up each pair of shoes, and we convinced Mom to let go of her cherished Spectators and high heels that were accidents waiting to happen if she ever wore them down the stairs at The Beach Club.

It seemed that she was game, offering blazers, sweaters, dresses, purses, and earrings to each of us. "Peg, take that sweater for work. I will look good on you. Lynn, how about that red blazer? Do you

~53~

want it? Kathy, take those black earrings but leave that Chico's skirt. I wear my Chico's all the time."

Oooh, how I wished that Chico's skirt would fit me... but no worries there. Mom was keeping that one, all swirly and sparkly with autumn-hued chiffon and sequins. She was the only one petite enough to wear it, no matter if the tags were still hanging on it from when we'd shopped for it three seasons ago.

My sisters and I returned home, arms laden with treasured finds, only to hear repercussions a few weeks later...

"Kathy, someone stole my red blazer. I can't find it anywhere. Who would do such a thing?"

After a quick update to my sisters, Lynn called Mom to remind her of our weekend and explain. She boxed up the now infamous red blazer and shipped it back to Mom via UPS. It was just too hard to compete with the pull from Mom's past.

"TV Is My Friend" (How I Acquired a Ninja without Really Trying)

When not engaged in Bingo using large-print cards – winning regularly – or dining in the café with her three table buddies, Mom increasingly spent a lot of time in her apartment watching TV. She positioned her 36-inch barstool close and to the side of the screen, so she could see figures out of the peripheral vision macular degeneration left her.

She said she liked the company.

She also liked the Home Shopping Network.

I found the evidence more than a few times on my now bi-weekly forays to The Beach Club. My usual routine was to gather and sort her mail from her lobby mailbox and recycle the newspapers stacked up on her counter. She ordered the newspaper, "so I can see what day it is." Then, I made the rounds to make sure her trash was emptied, her bathroom was clean, and she had a supply of the toiletries she needed.

One day, I spotted a rectangular, shiny foil box on her bathroom counter. The outside was lovely, but the inside...*Oh! the inside...* It contained the serum of eternal youth – Cindy Crawford Beauty, $80.00 initially, plus $39.95 in monthly recurring payments to replenish her supply. *What joy!*

"Mom, you're going to be 90 next June. What's up with the Cindy Crawford Beauty products in here?"

Still another visit yielded a Ninja blender, displayed in its colorful box on the counter next to her sink, accompanied by accessories, several cookbooks and vitamin guides. She ordered the blender, she said, because it afforded her the chance to eat healthier by juicing. No matter that The Beach Club provided three meals plus snacks daily, she couldn't read the directions nor the cookbooks and didn't know how she would carry home all the produce she needed from the grocery on The Beach Club bus.

Then, there was the Pan-of-the-Month Club. Mom had called the toll-free number and signed up for the Pan-of-the-Month Club. She didn't have a kitchen equipped with a stove. And she hadn't cooked in years. But these were copper-clad pans, lots of them, the latest in cooking technology. They came in two huge, heavy boxes, delivered to her door. I found them unopened in her living room, blocking access to her closet and her TV.

What the hell?! That was all I could think, while busy laughing my face off. I called all my siblings to recount this one. (When one of us brings it up, we still giggle.)

"Pan-of-the-Month Club?! How much did these costs, Mom?"

For a down payment of just $235 and a monthly installment of $29.99, she could keep the two skillets and, over time, equip her kitchen with the additional gems.

Holy shit, I thought, who talked her into this scam?

Mom's checking account was getting perilously low, so I paid for Cindy Crawford and her friend the Ninja out of our family funds and brought home the booty Mom couldn't use. It was a bit more complex, however, to unravel the pan fiasco, since they, too, were purchased with a recurring, automatic credit card charge. *I HATE those things!* I called the company and tried cajoling them into canceling, though they were having none of it. Finally, I raised my voice more than I should have, letting them know in no uncertain terms they were taking advantage of a blind, elderly woman. I threatened them with the Better Business Bureau, not that I knew what the BBB could do. That worked, though. Go figure. They promised to refund Mom's money and stop all future auto-payments. I packaged up the first installment of pans and shipped them back, on my dime, of course. But I kept the skillets. Heck, someone should get use out of them.

Yes, A Dollar is a Dollar...But Credit Cards are Free

Increasingly alerted to Mom's diminishing decision-making capacity, we sat down together once a month to go over her accounts. Those sit-downs were another revelation entirely.

I will never forget opening her credit card bill one weekend to find she had spent $2995 to upgrade her reading magnifier machine, only to hear her claim, "Well, it's only a credit card. I still have the cash in the bank, and besides, I get points toward airline miles when I use the card. I'll use the points to go to my nursing school May Breakfast Reunion."

This wasn't funny anymore. It wasn't pots and pans or beauty creams or juicers. This was more than troubling on several fronts.

First, why was the reading magnifier repairman in her apartment to service it in the first place? She was there alone, without me. How did she find him and invite him to her apartment? How did he talk her into trading her perfectly good machine for a new one, taking her old one with him when he left? How could he take advantage of her vulnerability by selling her an expensive, new piece of equipment he knew she depended on when all her old one needed was a new bulb?!

The fact that he had access to her and her credit card account really threw me. But almost as troubling was her defense of her decision. The cash was still in the bank, she said. And the credit card? Did she really think it was free?

Here we go again, I thought. Maybe it was just another little slip. I certainly hoped so, but this one didn't feel the same, at all.

How to Steal an Identity and Renovate a Fixer-Upper in One Easy Phone Call

My suspicions that Mom had become a scammer's mark were confirmed when I got a worried call from her at the office one spring afternoon. She rarely called me at work, so hearing her voice, I was alarmed.

She said she had received a call from "her bank" that afternoon checking on her account and asking her to verify her Social Security number, account number and PIN. They also asked her for her credit card number, expiration date and the 3-digit security code on the back. She called me because she wasn't sure she gave them the right information. She wanted me to call the bank back to confirm that they got all the information they needed. She said they told her if she did not confirm her account number, they were going to close her account.

Oh Boy! We were off to the races now!

It did not matter I was at work, this was an Identity Theft Emergency. Mom had no idea the implications of what might have transpired on that phone call. My first call was to the Fraud Department of Mom's bank. They put a stop on all accounts and referred me to the Credit Card Fraud Department. The Customer Service Representative was so helpful, thank goodness, because I was beside myself. *What if they drained Mom's already meager accounts? What if they used her credit cards and ran up huge bills? My name was on these accounts, too! Did this mess have the potential to wreak havoc with our credit?*

From Mom's bank and credit card records, the Rep could see that someone had used her credit card account in the name of a building company that very afternoon at a Lowe's Home Improvement store. The kicker, the business and the Lowe's were in Davenport,

Iowa. We were in Florida. This fraudster purchased goods to the tune of $4200.00 using Mom's card. Their purchases included a tub surround, laminate flooring, fence posts, chain link fencing, and a riding mower, all to be picked up that Friday at the store in Davenport.

My assumption after exploring all possibilities with the Fraud Department was that whoever made the original call to Mom to get her personal data, sold her account numbers through the dark web, then someone in Davenport bought them online. They ordered all the goods online, too, without ever having to show their face or confirm their own identity matched the card.

While the bank created a Fraud Alert on Mom's card, I got back on the phone to call the Davenport Lowe's to explain the situation. *Now that was one crazy phone call!* They thanked me for calling, but I could tell that the clerk at the store thought she had some sort of nut on the line. She quickly transferred me to the Store Manager so that I could recount the story all over again.

I never did hear back from the Davenport Lowe's to tell me if the perpetrator had been apprehended, though wouldn't it be just deserts if they got arrested when they showed up to pick up the goods? I could only imagine them trying to figure that one out. Who tipped off the cops? Oh, some middle-aged woman in Florida with a bee in her butt and a big score to settle. That would teach them not to my 90-year-old mother again! That would teach them! Well, probably not, but at least imagining my revenge made me feel better.

Once the accounts were secure again, at least a full day's work remained to unravel the snafu. Because Mom now had to vouch for her identity in person, I had to drive her to the local Social Security Office and to the IRS to alert them of the fraud. We had to go back to her bank to close those accounts and open new ones, reestablish her auto-withdrawals for her health insurance and her automatic deposits for her Social Security all over again. Both the IRS and Social Security provided her with PIN numbers that were to be used whenever we made any further changes (such as an address change or new bank account for auto-deposit). I also had to use the PIN when preparing and filing her taxes from that point on. One more set of numbers to remember from the growing list. *Sigh.*

One thing was certain. Mom could no longer hold her own financial and bank papers or credit cards in her possession. I bundled up all her financial records, check books, checks and registers, and the credit and debit cards and brought them back to our house.

She and I parted that day with a new understanding, or so I thought.

"Mom, you'll have to live on cash from now on, OK? We can drive over to the bank together whenever you need your supply replenished. I'll set up an account to pay the hairdresser here in the building in advance. You'll only need cash for tips and Bingo. We'll just go together on your errands from now on. It will be fun."

Old Stories Warm the Heart and Reveal the Soul

While out on errands like this, riding in the car with Mom, I often found it easy to engage her in questions about our childhood, her family, her relationship with Dad and her thoughts for her future. She talked of religion and of her grandfather. I was privileged to hear it all – the good, the thoughtful, the anxiety-provoking and the joyful. Bottom line…it was nice…two friends gabbing, getting to know each other better.

"You know, Kathy, my grandfather was a cement contractor who once owned many houses, including the one on Division Street we lived in growing up. He built that for Momma and Daddy when they were married in 1921. I think your cousin lives in it now. Grandpa also put in all the sidewalks in River Rouge. Your grandma told me he once turned down Henry Ford when Ford asked him to invest in his new business. Grandpa said no, thinking Ford was just a drifter with a dumb idea that would never amount to much. So –much for getting rich."

Really? Well, wouldn't that be cool if it were true, I thought.

If I could pose just the right questions, she talked of her own mother and siblings and her childhood friends –The Sophisticats– an exclusive girl's sorority she and her friends formed in high school. They even had their own sweaters, emblazed with a big red

"S" and a booth they claimed all their own in the soda shop across from school. Who knew my mom was a leader of the cool kids... something I never quite accomplished in my youth. She still kept in touch with them, those alive, anyway.

What I would give to have that sweater now!

She shared a lot during our errand days, things I had never heard and from perspectives I didn't know she had. She confided her joys and her worries about her family. From time to time, she talked of all the moves we made with Dad for his job, pulling up roots and heading to a new town, new school, new life every two years. She mused about the impact it may have had on us kids.

I assured her it had made me flexible, able to take on new situations without hesitation. But I knew it wasn't that way for all my siblings. For some, it gouged deep wounds, causing a life-long challenge and drive toward finding security. I guess, to be totally honest, it did that to all of us, really. I just didn't want her to know how hard it had been. Why ask her to take on that burden? We had all forged our own way, finding success in our own careers, security as best as we could define it and joy in our own families. She did not need to revisit decisions made long ago, in a different time. Why add to her already large compendium of worries?

Each of us kids had a different worry line in her brain, I think. Me, the cancer survivor, was I eating right; did I work too hard; was I too stressed? Peg, was she happy, lonely, was her car reliable enough for Michigan winters? Jill, all that way out in California, all by herself. What about her, Joe and their kids? Were they doing alright?

"You know," Mom said, "Dutch is a genius, and that Flannery – what an athlete! You know she made several baskets in her last game. She's smart too, just like Kate and Megan, Jay's twins."

When were Lynn and Lowen coming to visit?

"You kids should call each other more often. You need to be sure to keep in touch."

And Jay? Well, Jay...you could tell he held top rank in her heart like the youngest child often does. When was her only son, her baby, going to be promoted to President of Boeing?

"You know, Kathy, he is a genius, too, just like your dad."

It was hard to convince her to drop her worries. After all, we were all in our 50's and 60's by now. But a mom is a mom is a mom... forever...no matter how old her kids are. And I knew that, too.

As time went on, she also talked a lot about her nursing experiences. She had worked on a telemetry unit of a heart hospital until she was 72, when a fall at home one morning precipitated a need for extended sick leave, causing her to confess her true age to the HR Department.

That she continued to work because she loved it, not letting her age stop her is something I truly admire.

She talked at length about her health, her waning eyesight and the latest research on cures for macular degeneration highlighting for me her frustration with that dreaded condition.

"Kathy," she would exclaim, "there is a new clinic in Miami that is doing stem cell treatment...Germany has a new discovery... Now, they are putting telescopic lenses in eyes to allow people to read. You know, Kathy, our family has the most victims of MD of any other family in the University of Michigan study. I will have to make another appointment to get checked out there when I go to Michigan for the nursing school May Breakfast."

Her health and wish for a miracle cure were beginning to dominate our discussions more and more and more.

These discussions seldom strayed beyond day-to day-concerns or old memories. But once, on the car ride home after another visit to her beloved Internist, Dr. Canada, in which the doctor noted looming diabetes and a substantial weight loss, our chats touched a deeper, more sacred chord. We talked then of the end of life. She brought it up.

During that conversation, I found what I had suspected all along...Mom was afraid of dying. Now that she was growing into old age, she still held the belief that one could not go to Heaven without making it through Purgatory first. It was a Catholic thing. No wonder she was afraid of dying. She'd learned this idea in her Catechism days, and it had kept hold of her, regardless of how I tried to convince her of a loving, forgiving God the Father, one who certainly would not cause her to burn in Purgatory until our feeble Earthly prayers lifted her out of that temporary Hell.

No wonder she worried if Dad had made it to Heaven. No wonder she thought it essential to purchase a Catholic Mass from the Carmelite Sisters whenever one of her friends or an acquaintance or distant relative died.

If you aren't Catholic, these things may seem foreign to you, but to those of us in the fold (or "a lapsed Catholic" but devoted Christian soul, like me), it made sense she would think this way. Youthful impressions are often everlasting. These belief patterns were ingrained in her psyche. After all, her own mother Maude, Grandma to me, got up every morning at 4:30 to walk four blocks from her home on Division Street to Our Lady of Lourdes Catholic Church on the corner for 5:00 AM mass. Every. Day. Of. Her. Life. spring, summer, fall and even winter, to ensure peace and grace for all the departed souls of her loved ones. That kind of dedication makes a deep impression.

I remember, as a child of the 50's, kneeling with Mom and my sisters in a neighbor's house on Wednesday nights to pray the rosary, supposedly, as Mom recounted, to ensure the Russians would not cause a nuclear war with us. These things were essential to Mom and to her traditional family and way of life. Her Catholic faith was part of her identity. It was in the Milligan blood, and she was a Milligan through-and-through.

As we wrapped up that conversation, I committed in my own heart to opening that door again, should the opportunity arise. I vowed to assure her that once her time came, our loving Lord would embrace her and warmly welcome her home.

A few short months later, I would have that opportunity...

Mom's Path

Remember Mom's fierce spirit?

It was beginning to wane, though her body, conditioned by years of vitamins and walking five miles every day, hung on strong.

You could tell she increasingly felt out of her element. The world was so confusing to her now. People who were supposed to help only took advantage. Shopping on TV was convenient, but oh, those sales pitches. She got caught up in the possibilities, yet she increasingly lacked the discernment to protect herself from fraud. What once was her strength, managing her own finances, was betraying her.

Her vulnerability frightened her. She withdrew more and more into herself, staying home from The Beach Club shopping excursions, retreating to the safety of her family and small circle of friends. She sensed that big changes were happening inside her. It took all her energy to keep up with the demands of daily life.

Whenever she had visitors from out of town, she rallied, but then, once they left, she would sleep for days on end. Yet, she kept her friendships from earlier years active and her relationships with family thriving, including those with her younger sisters Eileen, Sally and Nancy, and her cousin Mary Jane. She spent long hours with them on the phone in the evenings. They knew her. They shared stories of long ago that refreshed her. It comforted her to keep up with their lives.

The spark and drive to connect and retain the essence of her being still burned hot.

My Path

At first, these incidents amused and irritated me. What was she thinking, I wondered. But then, they alarmed me. *What was happening to my mom?*

I knew she was no longer capable of handling her money; yet, who was I to take over? Wasn't she still full of vitality and insistent on her independence?

Caring for her was getting more and more complicated by the day, but I knew I had to step up. Helping her understand and accept her new limitations was an even bigger challenge.

I was cheerful and positive with her. I tried to keep my out-of-town siblings in the loop, sharing stories of the events occurring and attempting to convey my unease with the situations. Sometimes, though, it felt as if Jim and I faced each new development alone. But it was hard for anyone not involved on a regular basis to fully grasp the sort of changes we were seeing day-by-day, especially when Mom staged a rally whenever they came to town.

Their visits were infrequent, because all of us kids were still working full-time, though I was a few short months from retirement. Those rallies for company were not often required. It was a good thing, too. The aftermath wore Mom out. And, it wore me out.

I was out of my league. We all were. We just didn't know it yet.

Chapter Six:
Parallel Transitions – Parallel Transformations

One Foot in Front of the Other – Step by Step

D espite Mom's occasional lapses of judgment, life in our family was much more than just worries and surprises. Months turned quickly into years, going by at warp speed as we grew older ourselves.

At work, I was offered an early retirement buyout from my position at MacDill Air Force Base in Tampa, and I jumped at the chance to take the offer. It was a huge relief to offload that job in the world of military intelligence, a world I never knew existed when I accepted the position five years before. I was stretched far beyond my imagination in that role as a leadership trainer to civilians supporting those fighting alongside the military in Afghanistan, Iraq and against the drug cartels in Central and South America.

Before taking that job, I worked in HR at the Library of Congress Congressional Research Service and had been a Career Coach and Executive in an outplacement company and in colleges and universities.

What was I doing in a military environment, at the end of my career, no less?

The stress of swimming in that unfamiliar milieu had taken a toll on me. Just entering secure space in the building every morning, sitting down at my desk with three computers, one for unclassified data, one for Secret and one for Top Secret information, caused me to grind my teeth at night and unfortunately to resort to comfort food to dull the anxiety – packing an extra 50 pounds onto my small frame. Cheez-Its and Tic Tacs were my go-to lunch and dinner on nights I had to work late to hit ever-changing deadlines.

Despite the stressors, I learned more in those five years than I had in all my other jobs. This job was intellectually challenging as well as personally and professionally stretching. I knew now how to "fake it till I make it", learning an entirely new language of obscure military acronyms, and to stand in awe of the dedicated few who choose to serve the rest of us without flinching, no matter how perilous the duty.

Funny thing, this experience also shed new light for me on my upbringing. It opened my eyes to the makeup of my dad's spirit. He had volunteered as a Marine at 17-years-old, joining during WWII and rising to the rank of Captain before the end of the Korean Conflict. He loved The Corps. He never let us kids forget it, either. Though he never spoke explicitly of his service time, he expected obedience without question, taut corners on our beds each morning and immaculate mirrors as we scrubbed the bathrooms each Saturday throughout our childhood.

Each of us, in our own time and in our own way, escaped these military-style strictures, heading off to college or abroad, then onto marriage and families of our own. Yet, each year, on my birthday, I could expect a call from Dad with the familiar message, "Happy Marine Corp Birthday, Katydid."

Was it a coincidence I was born on November 10th, the same day as The Corps? Was it intentional (part of a much bigger plan) I landed in the heart of the military, Marines included, to gain a first-hand look at what drove these people to offer themselves in sacrifice to a cause?

I was blessed to know my dad at the end of his life. Working at MacDill after he passed away, I grew to better understand how he viewed the world and what may have unconsciously caused him to behave the way he did, the experiences that forged his personality from the beginning of his adulthood. He was a Marine. Seeing him in that way allowed me to see myself, my childhood and my mom differently.

Now I get it, Dad. Now, I get it.

Working as a civilian in a military operation changed my own heart, driving me to see and understand what it's like to try to be the salt and light in a dim and darkening world. It also showed me how ordinary people can happily live a life of sacrifice and service to others, above all else. It made my work caring for Mom seem light and easy, compared to all that my coworkers gave for all of us. Partnering with Mom in her care was a privilege. I have no reason to complain.

It might be hard to believe, but many of my co-workers wore their faith proudly and openly. Christian, Muslim, Hindu, Jewish, Catholic…it didn't matter. God brought me there for a reason. He had my growth in mind. Affiliating with a group of committed believers was new to me in a work environment. My colleagues took on life's challenges with grace, seemingly fearless, believing God had his hand in whatever occurred. I know the old saying, "There are no atheists in foxholes" sounds trite, but it was truer than I ever imagined.

There in that cube farm of Central Command, I was reminded to listen to God's Spirit and allow Him to lead. And I had a lot to learn about following. As my life became more closely entwined with Mom's, these lessons would be essential.

I thought I had bigger plans of my own. Oh, yes, now that my retirement date was set for January 3, 2015, I had big plans for my post-government life. I had a new job offer in hand. I was going to work with a local non-profit fighting Human Trafficking. And, I wanted to get back involved in politics – no longer restrained by the Hatch Act, prohibiting government employees from speaking out on issues.

Not that caring for Mom wasn't becoming more than a part-time job, I thought I could juggle both. And why not? I was juggling a lot now, wasn't I? Why not go to work doing something I really believed in?

"I, I, I." You hear that?

God had other plans.

But first, He allowed me to indulge my imaginings that I could drive this next stage of my life. Oh, I was so in control.

Can you hear God laughing? I think He still chuckles when He thinks of it. I know I do.

Searching for Mountaintops at the Seashore

Retirement. This was supposed to be the winter of my rebirth, or, at least, that's what I thought it would be. I enrolled in a class for Stephen Ministers, 50 hours of training led by my former pastor, intended for lay people who want to minister to those needing a friend and counsel. I accepted initiation into a local women's service sorority, an opportunity offered through a dear friend, Emily. And after a lot of prayer and angst, I turned down the job I'd been offered in a non-profit, certain I was not right for the role, opting instead to volunteer in their thrift store, selling high-end, used fashion.

The latter was fun. The Stephen Ministry training? That was challenging, yet, somehow, it spoke to me. It felt like I was readying myself for something.

In the first month or so after I left work, I said "yes" to everything. Once I got my bearings a bit and realized I had been trying to fill my emptiness with too many activities, not leaving time to breathe, or write or contemplate who I wanted to become now that I had the chance to reinvent myself, then I said "no" to much of it. It was like being a teenager all over again, but this time, with more experience to back me up. Rather than face what one of the books I read called "the liminal space between one stage of life and another," I had been striving to fill up all my space and time. I was testing out new experiences, but I was also running from the big hole that losing my work identity left behind.

Jim, ever the perceptive partner, sensed right away that I felt unmoored. I had been grabbing every random opportunity that came my way, but still felt like I was neglecting a "nebulous something" I professed vehemently I was being called to do. Trouble is I couldn't figure out what the Call tugging at my heart really meant, or how I was to fulfill it. I felt stuck.

One morning at the end of January, he offered me a respite – a weekend alone at the beach nearby in a room facing the ocean and sand. He booked me two nights at the Holiday Inn on Lido Beach. It sounds mundane, but it was my opportunity to contemplate and regenerate my soul. I jumped at the chance, packing up my journal and my laptop, intending to write, to pray and to meditate. It was time to figure out this retirement stuff.

I did write some, I did meditate, and I prayed, prostrate on the hotel room floor, brown shaggy carpet beneath my face, begging for guidance and direction. I needed to know my purpose. Actually, I just needed a purpose.

I needed to know I wasn't invisible, that my life still had meaning, that I still mattered in this unfamiliar world outside of work.

Walking the beach and listening to the waves, I tuned my brain to stillness, to the acceptance that only time would work out the meaning of what felt now like wilderness to me. It reminded me of my own cancer journey 12 years before, and the healing I did on the beach, when I had to trust, and wait, and believe that answers would come; when I had to believe that the future held promise that would unfold in Divine time, not my own.

I vowed then to live my life in daily practice, putting routines in place, honoring my own health and my commitments to family and my mom. I would wait and watch for what was in store for me next. I would stop trying so hard to control everything and just breathe.

Breathing proved a good and vital thing. I had lots of internal work to do. Hard work.

Walking with Angels

Finally, that February, I decided that in lieu of all the activities I took off my plate, I had to invest more in finding meaningful connections in my community. I needed women friends, especially now that Jim, working full-time from home, spent 8 or 9 hours a day on the phone conducting business remotely.

I had to get out of the house and give him space to get his work done. I had to get out of the house for my own sanity.

I could hear every word of his phone calls and feel every emotion coursing through him as he negotiated deals with big customers and strategized with his colleagues. Though I was delighted to have him home after living apart during the week for so many years, this was not what I expected.

Getting out of the condo was a must. I needed to find a life of my own making. I needed to balance out time with Mom with my relationships with others in my same life stage. Yes, I needed women friends.

So I reached out to two women I had met when we first moved back to Florida – Nancy and Emily – whose steady worldviews and delightful take on life added joy and laughter. I also participated in a small group through our new, local church – a large, multi-campus, non-denominational church we recently joined because Jim found a closer match to his faith. Through my initial foray into that community, I forged a deep friendship with Mary, a new transplant from the DC area. I introduced my friends to each other, and we began walking and talking weekly.

Our walks opened a door to sharing our own special knowledge of the road we now traveled together. We could often be seen striding through the streets of the subdivisions around us, laughing, solving each other's life dilemmas and egging each other on as well as holding each other up through celebrations and sorrows. Each was a relationship on-purpose.

On a personal basis, I began a more extensive workout regime and weight loss program. I established a discipline that did not fail me, rising every morning at 7:00, dragging on my yoga pants and the wicking T-shirts I found at Goodwill, then lacing up my shoes and heading out the door by 7:30. If I did not start my day that way, I would not get back to it. Soon, it became an obsession…a drive…a need.

My body craved to be active. But this was new to me. As a kid, I was the one who lingered long hours on the couch, reading books, daydreaming about the Beatles while munching peaches and potato chips. I was also the one who, until cancer, chemo, and menopause at 50, never had to think about my weight. Then, like so many others I knew, it felt like my body betrayed me. I was far from the athlete in my family. That role belonged to others. But I was determined.

At first, I could only walk a mile or two without getting winded. Then, though, I progressed to the weight machines at the club in our neighborhood. It was there I met my friend Susan, some 10 years my senior. I introduced her to Nancy, Emily, and Mary. For a season, we added Susan to our walking crew, enjoying her forthright personality and easy quips. She seemed so self-contained and confident. A nice match for our little foursome, now five.

Susan and I took to riding our bikes together through our neighborhoods every morning. I loved riding. It suited me. It touched something in me that felt like freedom. My body seemed more perfectly matched to the bike than it did to trudging along on my own. Once I started, I could ride forever. I could ride…and ride…and ride, emptying out my mind, thinking of nothing, praying to a God who felt closer than I had felt Him in a long time. Feeling the joy of wind on my face and the wheels spinning under me, I found bliss on that bike.

My companionship with Susan grew as we chatted on walks and our meandering rides. She talked of the challenges, pain, and exasperation of being the wife of a dear man of 80 with increasingly difficult dementia. He had been an industry titan, a legend in his field. A second marriage, he had wooed her, cared for her and loved her and her girls, always looking out for them. Now, she cared for him at home, savoring their remaining time together, working out strategies for whatever new struggles arose, honoring him for what independence and individual capacities he still retained. She showed so much respect for the man she loved, watching the spark of his spirit slowly winking out, yet loving him more.

I thought she was a rock, only occasionally broken by the weight of it all, steadfast and fierce in her dedication – another woman who could teach me to be fierce.

I offered empathy and understanding, though, at times, the part of me more full of opinions than knowledge broke through. I spoke often of my own care partner role for Mom and how the stress of it wore on my relationships with my family and taxed my understanding. When I got to feeling too sorry for myself, Susan offered compassion and sometimes a swift kick in the rear. She never gave the impression that my situation was not as difficult or heart-wrenching as watching her husband slip farther and farther away, though I knew it to be true.

We were from different upbringings and different times, and as far apart politically as you could get. Yet, we understood each other. I was hungry for her wisdom, ever a seeker of a different perspective to guide me through my transition. Susan was one of God's angels, sent to convey the wisdom I sorely needed. She did not disappoint.

Together, we created a tiny cell of support. We explored memory care and assisted living units in town and put our heads together to source and discuss the best local physicians and new treatment options for brain disease. Me? I offered an open ear and whatever knowledge I'd learned from my research and experiences with Mom that might be helpful. Susan offered a matter-of fact perspective on family life, advice on setting personal boundaries and persuaded me to lighten up my sense of guilt and obligation while also sharing an empathy hard-won through her own journey.

I am not yet sure that I have accepted and processed all she gave me. Susan says that if she offered a bit of advice a few times about how to handle an issue with Mom, and I kept doing the same old thing I'd been doing up to that point over and over, she would move on, certain I would get it at some later date. I wasn't ready for all she told me, so I hope she's right about that.

All the while my group of friends talked, walked and rode, we grew physically stronger. I was healthier than I had been in many years, and my spirit was, too.

These friends were my angels. I needed these women. We were present for each other in a way that only women can be, in keeping with others who went before us throughout the ages. My newly adopted sisters, all.

Hiking the Celery Fields: I'll Take a Hill Wherever I Can Find One

So, it was no surprise that I was intrigued when my real, younger sister Peg, called from her home in Holland, Michigan with a challenge...

She had healed from a knee replacement the fall before. Now, she wanted to walk a portion of the Appalachian Trail with her sisters in honor of her 60th birthday. She wanted to thumb her nose at her troubles of the past year and celebrate her new, post-divorce life. *Damn right!*

I wanted so badly to join in on her adventure, set for early October in Virginia. I could sense it. It would be a rite of passage for me, too. At first, I wanted to decline, fearful I could never keep up with Peg, Lynn (our fit sister) and Stacy (my brother's long-time love who also happened to have a fitness training business). I fought a huge battle of self-doubt. I felt like the slug in the group, despite my newfound physical confidence. I almost said no. But I could not stand the thought of being left behind. I did not want them to go without me. I wanted to be part of the Sisters Hike.

I vividly remember standing in the shower in our master suite, looking down as water dripped off the bumps and curves of my middle-aged body, thinking, "Damn it! Why can't I get out of my own way? I must do this. I WILL DO THIS. I'm all in!"

I called Peg. I said "YES! We're on!"

The preparations for hiking simplified my life. I put practically everything but Mom and prepping for the AT on hold. While Jim headed out for his Starbucks run each morning before settling down at his desk to field phone calls, I threw on my workout clothes and headed to the gym or my usual ride with Susan.

Soon, though, walking had to take precedence. I added longer and longer distances each week, wearing a small pack, loaded down first with 3 pounds of weights, then 5, then 10. At the advice of my sister, I bought trekking poles and pushed myself to longer and longer walks. I'm sure I looked ridiculous trekking through our flat, suburban neighborhood, poles in hand, pack on my back, sweat dripping first onto my headband then down my face and neck and fogging up my sunglasses, but I strode onward.

It took all morning every day. This was serious stuff.

To add challenge to my hiking chops, I sought out the only hills in town – either the driveway up to the clubhouse in my neighborhood, a laughable elevation change of at least 10 feet that I walked over and over again or, when I finally felt up to it, the Celery Fields in Sarasota, out past Fruitville Road, an old landfill transformed into a bird sanctuary and hiking park by the Selby Gardens Foundation.

The Celery Fields weren't a much bigger bump on the landscape, exactly 42.39 feet in elevation, but they were the biggest hills around. From up at the top of the steepest trail, you can see almost to the seashore. That trail, a thin ribbon of dirt worn into the grassy slope, really intimidated me. I did all I could to avoid it while eyeing other hikers enviously as they strode up to the highest plateau of the park. Some – the fit, young, ripped ones – even ran up and back down again without seeming to break stride or a sweat. "OK, that does it," I thought. "If they can do that, surely, I can tackle that hill. Nothing says I have to run up it like they do. I can stop halfway to catch my breath if I need to." *And I needed to.* But then, after a few more weeks, I didn't need to anymore.

I conquered the Celery Fields.

Caution - Downward Slope

Most afternoons, after a shower and a few chores, I drove over to check in with Mom.

Did she need anything? Did she want to go out for ice cream or to Walmart just to get out of the apartment? Sometimes she was eager. Other times, her response was listless and apathetic. Her world was shrinking. Still, when she was up to it, she relished hearing about the escapade we girls were planning.

"I'm so glad you and your sisters are finally going to spend time together. Too bad Jill can't join you, but she lives so far away. At least the rest of you will get close again," she'd say.

She was right. It was about time we broke down the barriers of distant geography and divergent life experiences. Each of us hoped that the Sisters Hike would help us achieve our unique personal challenges as well as bring us closer together than we'd been in years.

All the while we prepared for our grand adventure, Mom faced down her own set of challenges.

At times during my visits, I found Mom still asleep or lounging on her loveseat with her head propped up on a decorative pillow, neck at an odd angle, her eyes drowsy or closed. Her hair was mashed down and cockeyed on one side from the pressure of the pillow, a far cry from her fastidious past. She spent a lot of time this way now.

She was nearing her 90th birthday, a milestone worthy of a huge celebration. But as I was gearing up for my adventure, I could tell she was slowly wearing down. Oh, she still played Bingo every Wednesday night and sat rocking with her friend Ellen on the porch of The Beach Club after dinner, but she also slept a lot…a whole lot.

Her sleepy afternoons meant I could slip into her apartment quietly to pick up her laundry or tidy up before waking her. They also meant I could look around to see how she was managing during the hours I was away.

One essential change quickly became obvious. I had taken on the task of filling her daily pill box each week. A casual observer would think they were emptied each day as they should be. But I found many of the contents strewn on her bathroom or living room floor. Pills were in the sink, on the couch, under the table, on her bedside nightstand. *How many of her essential prescriptions was she missing each day?*

My more frequent presence at midday was a good thing, but I was not able to ensure she took her pills morning and evening, or even that she got up, showered and got dressed for lunch. Too often, I found her still dressed in her faded pink bathrobe, heedless the sun had risen past its prime. It was time to hire some supplementary care for Mom.

Mom's Path

As Mom's sight dimmed, so did her executive functions. Things like remembering which day it was, when to get ready for lunch or dinner, or how to be sure she took all her medications on schedule, fell by the wayside.

Any outside observer would not pick up on these newly developed deficiencies. But they were obvious to her family and to her closest friends. They were also obvious to The Beach Club housekeeping staff, who had to vacuum up the spilled pills and pick up the stray Kleenex strewn all over the floor of her apartment.

Her best friend Ellen called me aside during one lunchtime gathering. She told me that more and more often, Mom missed her meals and declined to join in the social time after dinner with friends on the porch. She thought Mom was relying on Boost, that chocolatey drink I frequently supplied to her as a meal supplement, to give her more protein. And, Ellen thought Mom was rapidly losing weight. She was right.

Mom's weight, which always hovered around 120 pounds, was now 101 pounds. She was wasting away – whether from apathy or some as yet unnamed ailment. It was time to intervene.

My Path

The other day as I was sitting down to write, and my recent conversation with Jack, my little grandson, came to mind.

We had just finished planting the flowers he selected for our miniature strip of a garden next to our condo's garage. He was exceptionally proud of the garden, all reds, pinks, yellows, purples and whites.

It was time to water when he stopped for a second, turned to me and said, "You know, Grandma, we have to take care of these flowers step-by-step."

"Yes, Jackson, that's right," I said.

"Do you know what step-by-step means, Grandma?" He continued, evidently with a message to share with me.

"You tell me, Jack, what does it mean?"

"It means first you plant them, then you water them, then you love them and help them grow."

Yes, Jack, I thought. That's what we all need, isn't it? Roots, nourishment, love and faith to grow.

Part III: Inklings Redux

Chapter Seven:
Back to the Future

Kim's Angel Care to the Rescue

K im was a lifesaver. Her company, Kim's Angel Care, was aptly named, that's for certain.

She came highly recommended by many of the residents at The Beach Club who were in her care. I contracted with her to check in on Mom every morning by 8:00, to lay out her clothes, encourage her to shower and go to breakfast and most importantly, to watch her take her morning medications. She or one of her other caregivers would circle back to Mom in the evening around 4:30 or 5:00 to remind her to go to dinner and administer her evening meds. They took daily notes, leaving the documentation for me to peruse, so I knew that someone had been there checking on her at least twice a day.

A friendship grew between Mom and Kim, though Mom hotly resisted a few of the other Angel Care staffers who came to help her. Mom called the other caregivers "part-timers" and often caused them grief, refusing to take her pills from them. She trusted Kim, so did I, but she was suspicious of the others, thinking they may be giving her the wrong pills or the wrong dosage, no matter how hard Kim and I tried to convince her otherwise.

A little paranoia was setting in. And something else was happening, too. Mom was beginning to drift in time.

The Past Becomes Clearer than the Present

Florida spring quickly passed into the heat of summer, though leaves had barely budded on the trees up north. By early spring, humidity and steady temps in the high 80's are the norm. For Mom, it was now too hot to venture outside during the heat of the day, so her couch time increased, and with it, her sleepy daydreams.

One afternoon I arrived at her apartment to find her perched on the edge of her loveseat wide awake, looking like the proverbial cat who had swallowed a canary. She sat straight up with a wide smile of pure joy on her face. Oddly, she also had an ace bandage wrapped expertly around her right ankle. The two did not seem to go together, so focusing in on the potential crisis first, I asked her, "Mom, did you hurt yourself?"

"Oh, yes," she enthused as if she was full of joy about that. "Clinton, my boyfriend, came to see me. We walked and talked for the longest time. Then, we stopped in front of the drugstore because I accidentally twisted my ankle. He asked me to sit on the park bench, and he wrapped it so lovingly. It doesn't really hurt anymore."

"Your boyfriend, Mom? I have never heard you mention Clinton before."

"Well, Kathy, he is such a gentleman. He is a great singer and piano player, too. The other day, he came and sang to me with my sister Nancy. I wore my long pink dress because we were going to get engaged. As I walked into the room, Nancy and Clinton sang the most beautiful song. It was the most beautiful music I have ever heard. When he left, he promised to be back for me soon."

"Mom, tell me more about this Clinton."

"Oh, Kathy. He is quite a love. He is a doctor. He works on the other ward at Providence, but he got assigned to my ward. The priest told me not to go out with him because he was an intern, and since I was a student, he could get in trouble for dating me. But we dated anyway. He was a wonderful dancer, too. We went out several times. He had to leave because he got called up in the war. We were going to get married when he got back, but he didn't come back after the war. This was before I met your dad. I am so glad he is back now."

This was the first time Mom mentioned anything like this. Not only had she claimed that this Clinton had taken her out for a stroll, but that he had wrapped her ankle and promised to be back for her. She did have her ankle wrapped, and when I checked with Kim, she said neither she nor any of her other caregivers knew about Mom's ankle. If they had, they would have noted it in their daily documentation.

So, who did wrap Mom's ankle? And, how did he sing to her with her sister Nancy?

Mom was close to her baby sister, Nancy, who was 11 years her junior. For years, they called each other every night to chat and connect. Nancy had died of pneumonia 7 months before Clinton's appearance. Mom and I had traveled to Michigan for her funeral in the depth of the past winter.

Mom must have been dreaming, I thought, still puzzled over the ace bandage.

"Mom, I am not sure Clinton is a real person. Why don't you let me check into it and let you know what I find out online, OK?"

"Well, if you do find out he's not real, don't tell me. I want to keep him around as long as I can."

Her reply stunned me.

It turns out that Clinton was indeed real. He was a physician who interned at Providence Hospital in the early 40's, just as Mom was finishing up her nursing school training there. He lived with his family in Dearborn, also just as Mom said. And, he was posted to the East Coast during WWII, then returned to the Midwest where he took up his medical practice in prestigious teaching hospitals in the Chicago area before moving in his later years to Kentucky or

Tennessee…I can't remember which one.

The thing is, this doctor was real, and he did live and work where mom said, but he died in 2005, 10 years before he came to walk with her and sing to her.

Was she reliving that time in a dream or fugue state, or was Clinton really here, singing for Mom with her sister Nancy, providing comfort through the veil that separates us from Heaven?

Finding his picture and profile online was surreal. As we drove over to see her doctor one afternoon soon after our initial conversation about him, I made the mistake of filling Mom in on all the research I'd found. I wanted her to share her story with Dr. Canada to see what she thought of this new development. Mom was glad to share it, but again she warned me, "Don't let the doctor tell me he is not real, Kathy. He might not stay. I want Clinton around as long as he can stay."

Mild Cognitive What?

So, we went to see Dr. Canada together. Mom loved Dr. Canada. She was always so caring, taking time to listen. As usual, Mom rose to the occasion on this visit like she did whenever conversing with anyone in the medical community

To hear her tell it, she was just fine, ate well, and was as active as a Senior Olympian, walking a mile every day through the halls of her apartment building. But she did agree when asked, that I could explain to the doctor my concerns about her true day-to-day activities and about the intensely real visits from people from her past.

Dr. Canada, always one to look at the positives, did not express alarm. She just chuckled when I mentioned the pans, the reading machine, and Clinton. Then she wrote out a referral for a good neurologist in the community, reminding both of us that Mom was beating all the odds by living into her late 80's. She said Mom could live well into her 90's if she kept up all her activities.

I just smiled. Why argue with such a positive assessment?

Oh, and Clinton? Mom never talked of him again.

The neurology appointment was set for two weeks after the Dr. Canada appointment. Between doctor visits, we maintained our usual routines, jaunting here and there on weekends and keeping up the chores. When we finally did get in to see him, he appraised Mom with a series of quick mental acuity tests, some which had to be bypassed because she could not see well enough to complete them. For example, who among us could draw a clock face with all the numbers in the right places when legally blind? I was glad I could accompany her for these evaluations and wondered what impact her visual impairment would have on the results.

When we met again for the outcome, the doc was encouraging. He said Mom had Mild Cognitive Impairment, but it should not impact her ability to live in her current setting, and, of course, that she should not drive. *No kidding.*

The doctor recommended she keep up her Tegretol (prescribed years and years ago when she had a seizure). He also encouraged her to add a trial of Aricept (one of the new drugs designed to help those with memory loss). Mom had high hopes for that med. She had always embraced trying out the latest treatment protocol for whatever ailed her. We filled the prescription with her favorite pharmacist then went out to lunch.

Nothing to worry about. That's what the doctor said. But he did not warn us about the squirrels...

Things that Go Bump in the Night

I got the first frantic call at 11:00 PM, a week or so after we visited the neurologist.

"Kathy, there is something in my room. Some sort of animal or flying squirrel. I was in bed, and it flew right by my head and bumped into my hand. It's hiding under the dresser. I can't see it, but I heard it swoosh by me. You have to come over! I can't sleep with that thing in my bedroom! Please come, quick!"

Jim and I leaped out of bed with adrenaline pumping, threw on some clothes and headed out the door. We just lived two exits down the highway, so at that time of night, our trip took only a few minutes. Mom was waiting for us on a couch by the door to The DeSoto Beach Club, wringing her hands, while Tom, one of the residents who sat up in the evening to let people in when they came back late from visiting, was trying to comfort her.

When she spotted us walking up to the locked door, she jumped up and rushed to let us in. "I'm so glad Jim came. He can catch that awful thing and get rid of it so I can sleep. But if he can't catch it, I'll have to come to your house. I can't go to sleep with a wild animal in my bedroom."

The three of us trooped up the sweeping staircase to the second floor and down the hall past the fire doors to Mom's apartment. Her door was wide open, evidence of her fearful, hurried exit.

She hung back in the hallway, still shaking a bit from her fright, while Jim searched every corner of her bedroom, bathroom and living room. He made a second sweep with Mom following behind, assuring her all the way that there really was nothing there.

"Maybe it ran out while you were downstairs, Mom," I offered. "Jim didn't find anything. You can sleep now. We'll sit here in the living room until you fall asleep, OK?"

An hour or so later, we tiptoed out of her apartment, careful to lock the door behind us. As Tom let us out into the warm late spring night, we puzzled over what had just occurred. Jim was certain Mom had seen a mouse. I wasn't so sure. Whatever it was, we hoped it was gone for good, along with the 11:00 alarms.

Time would tell...

Beware of Snakes

When I checked back in with Mom the next morning by phone,

she was much calmer. The things that had horrified her in the dark were not so scary by light of day. She joked about the incident but did mention that management had recently warned residents that there may be some wildlife stirring around the building due to some commercial construction and habitat destruction going on next door. Mom said they warned residents to watch out for snakes.

Well, she was ready for snakes.

The next time I visited her that week, I noticed an unusual odor in her apartment. *Was that mothballs?* I remembered the smell from my childhood when they were the go-to deterrent against moths eating holes in fine woolens between seasons. I didn't know they were sold anymore, but Mom apparently found some on her last trip to Walmart on The Beach Club bus. They were strewn around her apartment like little white, sparkling jelly beans, tucked in every corner and under every piece of furniture. *What a stink!*

"What is that smell, Mom?"

"Just mothballs, Kathy. Ellen told me snakes don't like the smell of mothballs. They'll stay out of my apartment for sure, now."

"Mom, they stink, and you are on the second floor. How would a snake get up here anyway? Besides, these are dangerous. What if Jackson mistakes them for candy? This makes no sense, Mom!"

But I could not dissuade her. I left the mothballs for the time being, along with her delusion that snakes could invade at any minute, vowing to surreptitiously remove them, one-by-one when she wasn't paying attention. It took me another week to find them all.

Mom's Path

To Mom, it made perfect sense that vermin could invade her apartment, since even Management at

The DeSoto Beach Club had warned of potential trespassers from the construction site. Not the human kind, but those that can sneak up on you in the dark. It also made perfect sense to try a home remedy, one her best friend recommended and was most likely one her own mother had used in days gone by to rid the house of bugs and varmints of the unsavory kind.

But when she perceived whooshing air and thumping sounds in her bedroom, it also frightened her, especially since her failing sight heightened her other senses and her fears of the unknown and unexplained. How long would she have to wait for us to catch that elusive flying creature?

What did not register with her or me at the time was that these sensory events could be illusions, perhaps stimulated by chemicals in the Aricept, her newest medication. None of us caught that right away…

My Path

As I think back on this time with Mom, I remember vacillating a lot between thinking she was losing her mind and that I was overreacting to her occasional lapses in memory and her "daydreams".

Truthfully, I was intrigued and fascinated by the visit from her old boyfriend and her sister. The idea of someone coming to comfort her with song from beyond our visual world comforted me, too. I have always had a sense that Heaven and our Earthly existence were more intertwined than we know. Since feeling so many spirit-filled touches myself during my cancer experience years before, I was primed to accept as real what others write off as delusion. So it was easier for me to treat these events as curiosities, rather than medical emergencies.

The real emergencies would come soon enough.

Chapter Eight:
Milestones and Joyful Days

O ur lives were not all training routines, late-night squirrel escapades and errands and doctor runs with Mom. That winter through early summer, excitement was growing along with our family as our oldest son Mark got engaged to Terra, bringing the joy of two new grandchildren (Natalia and Rocco) into our lives.

Mom was thrilled, too. She loved a good party. She loved weddings. And she loved our guys and loved her great-grandchildren. Two more were a bonus gift. As soon as she learned about the wedding, she wanted to shop for a dress. Mom was always thinking about the right attire for every event. You gotta love her!

Terra came from a small, tight-knit family, and we were eager to get to know them better. That they lived at such a distance in a suburb of Detroit didn't make building a relationship easy, but The Cottone's certainly held their arms open wide to us. It was like we were family already.

Thanksgiving celebrations at The Cottone's would soon become holiday traditions in the new Flora household. We were quickly drawn into their laughter, the enticing aromas and tastes of their savory Sicilian cooking and the cacophony of relentless trash talking in frenetic (and now traditional) Wii bowling tournaments. We were in love with all of them!

Thank goodness for my sister Peg, my brother Jay and Stacy, who gladly came to Florida, staying at our condo to celebrate the holiday with Mom, creating new traditions for her to look forward to each year. We needed to know she wouldn't be alone on the holidays, and we needed the break. It was important for my siblings to spend time alone with her, as much as it was important for us to get away from time-to-time. Their kindness made it possible for Jim and me to have a bit of respite and to focus on our son and his new family, too.

Keenly aware that our small nuclear family was quickly evolving, I suggested to Jim that we try to take one last Flora Family vacation with our guys before the wedding. So, we planned a trip to Charleston, South Carolina. I called each of the boys to propose they join us on the trip scheduled for summer 2015. They were in.

But it wasn't five minutes later that Mark called back and said, "Hey, Mom, we want to go to Charleston. But what would you think if we got married while we were there? Terra has always dreamed of getting married in Charleston. Do you think it would work?"

Are you kidding! We were delighted beyond words.

The date was set – August 25, 2015 (4 days after Mark's 35th birthday). The timing is only significant to my own Momma Heart, because he always said as a teenager, "I'm not getting married till I'm 35!" His vehement declaration always made me chuckle. He was right, after all.

With venue and date set, the rest of the logistics remained to be arranged. Since Jim and I planned to rent a 3-bedroom house for our small family's vacation, we decided to ramp up the specifications and search for somewhere that would accommodate all The Cottone's and The Flora's and a possible stray friend or cousin or two. We found that the vacation rental homes on The Isle of Palms perfectly fit the bill, pending Terra and her mom's final approval, of course.

The three of us girls – Terra, her mom, Connie, and I – traveled to Charleston for a few days in March to confirm the choice. Knowing I would only be going overnight, I didn't tell Mom I was going out of town. I worried, knowing that Jim was also out of town on business, but maybe she wouldn't even miss me. I struck out on my solo road trip, excitedly putting miles behind me and my day-to-day cares, daydreaming about the biggest event in our family's history since our guys were born.

Maybe, just maybe, my worries about Mom were unfounded.

For that first afternoon and the next morning before starting my drive home, I reveled in Charleston's mystical charms, while thoroughly enjoying the time away from the duties of caring for my mom. For just a few hours, I got to talk with my new daughter-to-be and her mom about dresses, and venues and romantic, girly things. *What a joy!*

Out of the Reverie, Back into the Fire.

The mystical spell that was Charleston was soon broken.

I wasn't even 10 miles out of town on my return trip when my cell phone rang with an alarming call from Kim, Mom's morning and evening caregiver. Mom had taken a fall getting out of the shower that morning and was in the Emergency Room of Lakewood Ranch Hospital. Kim had called an ambulance, suspecting that perhaps an incident of low blood pressure caused the fall. Besides, she wanted to be sure that Mom had not sustained a concussion.

This was the first time Mom had ever fallen, except once in The Villages years ago when she tripped and missed a step out to her lanai, so this was a frightening new development.

Kim didn't know the exact circumstances causing Mom to take the tumble, but she didn't want to take any chances. The hospital staff was doing tests, with no diagnosis yet. I was needed as soon as I could get there. By policy, neither Kim, her staff, nor the staff at The Beach Club was allowed to accompany residents to the hospital. Besides, I held Mom's Medical Power of Attorney, along with my sister Lynn, who lived 1200 miles away. I was the only one who could authorize further treatment if any was required.

I drove back as if my own life depended on it. I made it all the way to the hospital in just 7 hours and 50 minutes, taking no stops except to pee along the way.

We were lucky this time. Mom's bruises on her elbows and hands looked bad, but she hadn't sustained a concussion or any broken bones. The Emergency Room Doctor released her with the admonition to rest for a few days, then to be more careful. Rather than risk another more serious injury than her hurt pride and a few nasty bruises, she was to use a cane or a walker if she felt unsteady on her feet. I took her home to our condo and settled her into our guest room for the night. I wanted to keep an eye on her for a while before letting her return to her own place.

But she was having none of the cane and walker stuff. "I'll be just fine, Kathy. This fall was just a fluke. I'm not going to use a cane, for God's sake. Those are for old farts!"

This, just two months from her 90th birthday.

The Party – Princess for a Day

Despite this setback, I had something up my sleeve. Jim and I were hosting family and friends for a big 90th Birthday Bash. We weren't going to let a little fall stop us, and Mom seemed to recover quickly.

We encouraged everyone she knew, whether able to attend or not, to share photos they had for a photo book and slide show highlighting her life.

Family members made special arrangements to travel, including at least half the grandkids, while two of Mom's sisters planned to come down together from Michigan for the occasion. Mom's best friend Ellen and I plotted how to keep the secret from Mom. "Hush", I told them all, "This is a huge surprise."

Late the afternoon of her party, as the guests began to arrive, I put the finishing touches on the tables, putting out place cards and a birthday crown and scepter for Mom to wear, princess for the evening, marking her place of honor between her sisters and her best friend Ellen.

My favorite memory of that evening is of Mom, a broad smile on her face, Jack on her lap and her crown askew. Yes, she was loving it, every bit of it. She was indeed Princess For a Day, just as we all intended.

During her birthday weekend, it seemed Mom regained her equilibrium, both physically and mentally. Her delight in having her family together brought out her best, her face shining in joy and her eyes sparkling bright.

As we carted the gifts and cards, along with her plastic, bejeweled crown and scepter up to her second-floor apartment that night, I thought, what a night! What a perfect weekend! Perhaps she is alright, after all. Maybe the periodic incidents of odd behavior were just that...periodic incidents of odd behavior to be shrugged off as quirky one-offs in an otherwise unremarkable existence.

What other 90-year-old did we know who was doing so well? I think I was joined by all my siblings in our own hopeful assessment, what the Catholic nuns from our childhood memories used to call "wishful thinking."

I was too proud of what we had pulled off to think any other way. I hoped everyone went to bed smiling that night. I know Jim and I did...exhausted but smiling.

Mom's Path

You know that old Beatles' song "In My Life?" It was Mom's favorite. It speaks of memories of places gone but not forgotten, of people, and things...you know the one. Celebrations were always Mom's thing. She loved a party. She loved hosting family and friends for the holidays, sometimes seating 20-30 people in her dining room, with the overflow at card tables set up in the adjoining living room, the kids in the kitchen at our wooden table.

Mom was a hostess, and holidays were her thing. Birthdays, too. We never had a birthday while we were growing up that she didn't bake one of her signature cakes with homemade buttercream frosting, indulging us by letting us have cake for breakfast the day after our celebrations. I can still taste it.

Even with her increasing blindness and on and off delusions, decorations on her door at The DeSoto Beach Club had to reflect the changing holiday seasons. And, her small Christmas tree was essential during the biggest of holidays. She kept her gilded ornaments from our days as teens packed away in her closet, and on the Friday after Thanksgiving, she bedecked that little tree until its artificial branches drooped.

Knowing that Jay and Stacy and Peggy would be joining her for Thanksgiving, then helping her decorate her apartment for Christmas got her spinning plans for the celebrations, though she could not follow through with most of them. But the anticipation of a Thanksgiving with her kids, her birthday party, and a wedding in the not-too-distant future gave her something to look forward to, something to dream about when her days grew long.

Mom was delighted. After all, she was going to a party.

My Path

Knowing how much Mom valued tradition and celebration made it important for me to continue these holiday traditions with her. Jim and I both felt a commitment to make sure we included her in all our birthday parties, Christmas Eve dinners and the gift opening free-for-all that is Christmas morning with grandkids. She came alive those days, more than at any other time.

We'd go out together to Lowe's or Walmart to scout decorations, or get gifts and cards, gift bags and ribbons. Then, we'd spend hours wrapping, talking and reminiscing.

We'd sit together with a glass of Baileys on Christmas Eve, lights turned low, Christmas tree sparkling and talk of our memories. She'd chuckle at my stories of stepping on a tack while hanging my stocking on her mantle as a kid, and I'd smile when she remembered Dad's homemade eggnog, a concoction of raw eggs and ice cream that would draw the shame of the health police for its caloric content and its potential for salmonella – something we only think of today, not in those more innocent times.

I learned so much about her in the quiet of those evenings – about her own grandfather, of her Mom, sisters, childhood friends and her memories of Dad. I cherish those simple days together. She was the anchor in our little family.

That's why it was so important for me to throw her a 90th birthday party, and why Jim so readily agreed. I wanted to make this milestone birthday one she would always remember – with friends, family, party hats and streamers, cake, flowers, and crowns. We were going to throw her the biggest bash ever.

Mom was 90, and she deserved a party!

Chapter Nine:
What the Mind has Wrought

One Wednesday evening a few weeks after the party, long after everyone had returned to their homes and routines, Mom called, her voice frantic. The flying malevolence that had plagued her in the spring was back again.

After a joyful stretch of normality, months without it stalking her, she was desperate to escape the fear she felt as she perceived its presence following her with fiery eyes from its hiding place under her dresser.

"Kathy, I can't stay here. I have to come to your house or I won't sleep at all tonight. Can I sleep in your guest room? Come get me, please! Please hurry! I can't be in this apartment with that thing hiding under my dresser and thumping around all night long."

What could I say? Of course, she could come stay the night. We had planned to go shopping together in the morning anyway. I was increasingly focused on preparations for Mark and Terra's wedding. And since we planned for Mom to join us in Charleston, I wanted to take her to buy a dress to wear to the rehearsal dinner and another for the wedding itself, now just a few weeks off.

As I answered her fear with as much calm as I could muster, I am ashamed now to say that my first thought was how much more convenient it would be for me to have her here in the morning. It was better than driving the 15 miles to her place then backtrack to the stores in which we planned to start our dress search tomorrow. I dismissed the animal fear as something I hoped would pass as usual, or maybe even as soon as she was settled down the hall from us in our condo.

Holding back a sigh I replied, "Sure, Mom, I'll be right over. Be sure to pack some PJ's and wear your sandals so you'll have them when we shop in the morning. Just gather your things and head down to the lobby. I'll be right there in a few minutes to pick you up. I'm certain that whatever you are hearing will be gone tomorrow. And I promise to call the office to schedule an exterminator to check things out."

An hour or so later, with her snuggled under the coverlet in the guest bed, the hall bathroom light streaming into our guest room, I crawled back into bed myself. "She should be OK in the morning," I murmured to Jim as he rolled over to check the time on his phone.

It was 12:45 AM, way past my bedtime. I knew I would be dragging in the morning. Even more so when I awoke a few hours later to sounds of Mom wandering around in the kitchen, searching cupboards and the refrigerator for what I assumed was candy or ice cream. Apparently, sleep was more elusive than either of us anticipated.

I stumbled out of my room to check on her to find that "that thing" still had her in a panic. What seemed like perhaps a squirrel, mouse or bat when it first showed up in her room at The Beach Club became even more ominous when she felt it had followed her to our place. She heard thumps on the bedroom wall, whooshing past her ear as she cowered under the covers. The devilish, sinister threat left her shaking and disoriented.

"Why won't it leave me alone, Kathy?! Why did it follow me here? Why can't I get away from it?"

"I don't know, Mom. But I do know that you are safe here. I'll sit with you until you fall asleep," I assured her, feeling much like I was comforting a toddler who imagined a ghost in the corner or a monster under their bed.

I held her hand as I rocked softly in the rocking chair I had placed near the head of the bed for nights when I could rock our grandson, Jack, to sleep. Soon, she was snoring quietly. I tiptoed down the hall and back to bed, my heart aching for her, unable to wipe away the terrors conjured in her head.

Morning Brings Relief – Or Does It?

When Jim's alarm went off the next morning, I rolled out of bed. He was already up and on his usual morning Starbucks run when I looked in on Mom. Still sleeping, still snoring.

I had time to go for a walk before she stirred awake after a harrowing night. Dragging on my workout gear, I took off at a brisk pace around our neighborhood, praying with every step, "Lord, help me know how to handle Mom's fears. Help me know what to do." That prayer became my mantra as I planted my hiking poles and circled our subdivision, shaking off my fatigue while waiting for God's grace to come.

What came to me was a memory of a coping mechanism that had worked for me years ago. As a person for whom anxiety was a constant companion for a time in my early 20s, I knew it could quell persistent fear and quiet a mind racing with "what if's." I would "act as if" with Mom. In other words, I would treat her as if all was well, as if whatever she saw, whatever she was feeling or imagined was real…because it was real to her.

I would walk beside her throughout this day, focusing her attention, and mine, on ordinary daily activities, things that got her moving out in the world and out of the house. We would act as if everything was normal. We would focus on ordinary things that would anchor her to reality and help her feel normal by doing, thinking about and talking about real, normal things.

"Yes, this was a good path forward," I thought out loud. "It helped me through my anxious times, step-by-step, day-by-day. Maybe it will help Mom, too."

Thinking she might be up by now, I hurried back from my walk.

She finally awoke around 10:30, wandering out of the guest room to the smell of fresh coffee brewing and her favorite peanut butter toast waiting for her on the counter.

"Come and sit by me, Mom. Let's figure out our day. I made your coffee and your toast. Are you hungry for breakfast?"

I didn't bring up the incidents of the night before, wondering if she even recalled any of it or if it had faded like nightmares do when chased away by the dawn.

Wondering would have to take a back seat to my plan, though. Mom and I were going shopping. What more normal activity could two women do together? We were going to find her the perfect dresses. But first, showers, then we'd be off.

My prayer was that I could touch Mom's spirit with grace and calm now, as she had touched mine so long ago. Yes, we were going shopping.

Mom's Path

Night was a particularly fearful time for Mom. It was the time when darkening shadows fell across the room, when quiet fell within her building and the stillness amplified the occasional creaks, whooshes, and groans that arise in any building, or in one's imagination when not otherwise occupied by diversions such as TV or a good book.

Mom's equilibrium had been teetering on a knife edge for a few weeks. Although it was usually only evident in one-off comments about the need for exterminators, or the more frequent requests for late night visits, if I had looked more closely at the patterns of her conversation and behavior, tracking the changes evident, I may have better anticipated that a break was coming.

Not only was her mindset more on edge, she was also complaining more about physical symptoms. "My eyesight is getting worse, Kathy," she'd say. "Things are not clear today." Or, "I am so constipated, Kathy. I am so very, very cold, Kathy. I just can't get warm. I just can't go. My face is twitching so much. I have to get to the neurologist. Maybe I need my Tegretol adjusted."

All these comments, coming more and more often via phone calls or in my now daily visits, were indicators she was growing more uncomfortable in her skin. Uncertainty plagued me. I wish I could have stopped the onslaught.

But my wishing didn't make it so. It just didn't work that way.

My Path

As I walked, pondered and prayed for guidance about Mom's fearful night, my own experience with fear rose out of the deep reaches of my consciousness. I recount it briefly here, because out of that experience also rose deep compassion and an empathy for Mom, borne of gratitude for her steady presence during that time in my life. How long it took for me to need the lessons I learned. How grateful I am for them now, as I seek to comfort her fears. Here is what happened to me then...

Years ago, as a Freshman in college, I experienced a life-altering crisis that brought me to my knees, filled with anxiety and fear. To put it in the rawest terms possible, someone tried to kill me.

I was dating a man several years older than my 19 years. He was controlling and manipulative. When I attempted to break away from the relationship, running away from him to attend a different college in a different town, he stalked me.

One Friday night, right after Thanksgiving, he drove his car at high speed into a building. I was the passenger in that car. After the crash, I barely escaped the pummeling blows he rained down on my head and face. By God's grace, I did break away, stumbling out of the smoking vehicle and running into the night, screaming in fear, pounding on the front door of a house on the corner. A bewildered couple took me in, calmed my shock and allowed me to call my parents. They must have been panicked themselves at the spectacle of this wild-haired girl shrieking on their doorstep at 2 AM. Their warmth was a much-needed salve to my panic.

That my mom was somehow connected to my fearful spirit, jolting awake in her bed miles away when it happened, is a miracle. That night is when I learned she had a knack for intuitive connection with those she loved. She never made too much of it as we were growing up. But it served us then and serves me now, a spirit gift she passed along to me.

The other gift she gave me, as I struggled to

regain my footing during that horrific time, was the gift of practical, matter-of-fact love. She encouraged me to "act as if" until the anxiety passed. "I understand you're scared," she'd say. Then, rather than talk about what had just happened, she encouraged me to move, to get up, to get going. "Come on, the whole family is going ice skating. I want you to join us. It will do you good."

Somehow, she sensed that to be engaged outside of my fears, doing something that anchored me to the physical world, would allow my mind and body to come back into alignment.

I rarely think of that time in my life, but the lessons learned then were essential now. Mom was right about "acting as if." It was the same strategy I employed with her the morning after her fears returned. Because I had once experienced soul-crushing fear and grinding, buzzing anxiety, I knew how those painful emotions can undo a person. I also knew what could soothe and calm those beasts; a tender hand, warm touch, matter-of-fact love, and an activity to anchor one to reality.

The Fall

I helped Mom get set up for her shower in our guest bath, the typical second bathroom with a sink, toilet, and tub/shower combination. I put down the bath mat, gave her two fresh towels, some body wash, shampoo and toothpaste, then closed the door softly, leaving her to her own morning rituals.

I jumped into the master bath shower, hurriedly washed and dried my hair and selected a sundress and sandals for our shopping trip. It was then that I heard a loud THUMP followed by Mom's pleading cry, "Kathy, help me! I fell…Help me!"

"Holy Crap!" I came running from my bedroom. This can't be good, I thought, and it wasn't.

When I attempted to get to her by opening the guest bathroom door, I found her wedged between the tub and the cabinets, blocking me from opening the door more than a few inches, her head resting at an odd angle near the sink, her body wrapped awkwardly inside the fallen shower curtain.

She seemed dazed, so I had to speak loudly and firmly. "Mom, can you get up? Scooch over if you can. I can't open the door to get to you. If you can move just a bit, I can get in and help you up." My heart was pounding, orders and questions tumbling rapidly over each other, "What happened, Mom? Do you think you broke anything?"

Finally, she was able to shift her body slightly, just enough to allow me to slip through the partially open door. I stepped over her, searching for a better-leveraged position to help her up. Together, we struggled, but she was able to regain her footing.

I wrapped her in a towel, then her fuzzy pink robe. "Here, sit on the toilet seat, Mom. Let me check you out. Do you think anything is broken? What happened? How did you end up outside the tub?"

In the minutes that ensued, we came to the conclusion that while standing in the shower, she felt dizzy and grabbed onto the shower curtain for balance. The tension rod holding up the shower curtain gave way, sending her and the curtain tumbling over the edge of the tub and onto the bathroom floor. She struck her head on the counter top, which explained the pebble-sized welt rising on her forehead. But that didn't explain the dizziness.

After careful examination, we determined she didn't have any broken bones. She was shaken up a bit but insisted on getting on with our day.

Really, Mom?

"OK. Let's sit for a minute, then get dressed. If you still feel like going, we'll go. But you have to tell me if you're still dizzy and don't feel like it. That fall shook you up pretty good."

Thirty minutes later, we're in my SUV, heading toward Beall's, a great source of summer dresses of all types, from fancy lace numbers that were all the rage, to flowery, flowy ensembles that would be suitable for a beach wedding in the heart of summer in the Deep South. If she was still game for shopping, so was I.

It puzzles me that I didn't even think to call her doctor right away to report the fall, just taking her word for her physical state, focusing more on the fact that her state of mind seemed clearer and more in touch with reality than it had been the night before. *What was I thinking?* I was following my prior plan, trying my best to handle what came, taking my cues from Mom and her behavior.

As I look back, I realize my best wasn't nearly enough.

Blue Dress, Green Dress, Striped Ties and Pink Trees

We walked across the hot parking lot and into the store together, Mom holding onto my arm as she learned to do in her classes for the visually-impaired. Once in the store, she transferred to the shopping cart for stability, strolling beside me toward the dress aisles.

The layout of Beall's is that of a wide, one-story box store, with aisle after aisle full of colorful Florida styles. So, it didn't register with me at first when Mom exclaimed "Kathy, look at those colorfully striped ties. I bet Jim would love one." We weren't even close to the Men's Department. There were no striped ties anywhere near us. Still, she was seeing striped ties.

So, I set my original plan to "act as if" into action. "Come on over here, Mom. We can look at ties later. Let's find you a dress. How about this green lace, sleeveless sheath? I bet it would look pretty on you, and it's dressy enough for the wedding. Oh, and how about this blue, flowery one? It's delicate and just great for the beach rehearsal dinner."

Let's anchor back to reality, Mom. "Why don't you try these on?"

Both dresses were a perfect fit. Mom pirouetted in front of the mirror, though she could only see a shadow of her reflection around the periphery of her vision.

"Those look beautiful on you, Mom!" I assured her.

She agreed.

Now for shoes, purses, and jewelry to set off the ensembles. Beall's had a department for all of these things, the reason I chose it as our shopping destination in the first place. We selected a new pair of white, low-heeled sandals with silver accents for the green dress and silver slippers for the blue one. I had to steer her away from the heels, knowing that the uneven surfaces of the wedding venues (beach sand and then rough brick pavers) would pose an issue in anything but flats.

As we approached the costume jewelry, her vision changed. "Kathy, that is so weird. When I look at the jewelry and turn my head, the displays follow me. I can still see those necklaces clearly. They are still there. Look," she said, a puzzled expression on her face as she reached her hand out in front of her, fingers grabbing at the air as if to grasp an object. "Can't you see them right in front of me?"

She didn't seem frightened, just bewildered. *What was causing this odd manifestation?* Me? Well…I was frightened. Did her fall this morning damage something in her eyes or cause more than a simple bump on her head? I had to get her home.

We quickly made our way through check-out and back to the car, Mom marveling the entire way home about a variety of colorful objects floating in and out of her line of sight.

That we actually waited in the checkout line and bought the two dresses, shoes and accessories rather than leaving the store immediately empty-handed astonishes me now. But remember, I was in "act as if" mode.

About a mile from home, she exclaimed, "Kathy, watch out for those pink trees! There, in the middle of the road. Watch out! You're going to hit them!"

I knew we were in for it. Something was desperately wrong with Mom. I had to call her doctor. As I think back now, I wonder why I didn't drive right to the emergency room of the local hospital rather than back to our place. It was only about 5 miles in the opposite direction from our condo. But that wasn't a choice that even crossed my mind at the time, foolish as it seems in hindsight.

Our condo is on the second floor, so I helped Mom carefully navigate up the stairs and into the living room. "Why don't you just rest here on the couch while I call Dr. Canada to see what she thinks of these visual disturbances, OK?"

I propped her up on some pillows, draped the afghan over her shoulders and dialed the doctor's office. When the receptionist finally answered, after what seemed an interminable stretch, she listened for a quick minute to my explanation of what had happened and told me to hang up and dial 9-1-1.

Whoa, I'd never had to do that before for someone I loved.

The dispatcher asked several questions, then advised me to make sure our door was unlocked and to wait in the driveway for the first responders to arrive. "It will take a few minutes for them to get there, so go check on your Mom first," she instructed.

Mom was sitting straight up, staring at the wall in the great room, exclaiming, "Oh, look, Kathy. Do you see that dog? He is coming out of the wallpaper just above the TV."

We don't have a dog or wallpaper.

"Look at those soldiers. I think they are gathering to hear that general give a speech. See them over in that corner?"

"What pretty flowers! They are everywhere. Can you see them? They are just like the ones in our planters in front of the house in Little Falls. I bet they are blooming just for us," she said, her hands reaching out to grasp what only she could see, images scrolling faster and faster as her mind struggled to keep up with the movies flashing in front of her.

Then, I heard the siren. I left her sitting there and scrambled down the stairs and out to the driveway to direct the emergency crew to our door.

A fire truck was the first to roll up as I stood near the garage door, waving it in. The paramedic hopped out of the front seat and asked what seemed at the time to be a crazy question, "Is this call for you?"

What?! For me? Of course not!

"No, ma'am," I returned to my Defense Intelligence Agency military parlance to address the paramedic. "My mom had a fall this morning, and the doctor wanted me to call 9-1-1. She started hallucinating and seeing some crazy things but otherwise seems okay. She did have a blow to the head when she fell out of the shower and has a small bump on her head. By the way, she is 90 and is legally blind with Macular Degeneration."

For some reason, I was embarrassed they thought I would have called 9-1-1 for myself then wait in the drive for a ride to the doctor. *Sheesh, who does that?* Later, when I recounted the incident to our nephew, Doug, who was a firefighter/paramedic, he said it was common to be called out on a fire or medical call for reasons having nothing to do with medical emergencies. *Really?* Well, at least that explained the odd question from the first responder.

We stood in the drive for just a moment, awaiting the ambulance and crew arrival. Once there, the paramedics offloaded a stretcher and followed me up the stairs to the living room. Mom was expecting them, and although still distracted by her visions, she was able to answer all their questions, designed to assess her orientation to reality. She passed.

They told me they would be transporting her to the hospital and asked which one I preferred. Mom had been to Lakewood Ranch Hospital in the past, so it made sense to take her there.

"OK, Mom, I'll follow the ambulance. See you there in just a few minutes."

They rolled her up to the ambulance's back door and into the waiting vehicle. No more sirens or lights on the way out of our neighborhood. Apparently, my personal alarm at her odd hallucinations wasn't met with equal alarm by the professionals who conducted an initial assessment. But regardless, it was important for her to be seen in the ER, just in case she'd experienced a concussion or broken bones in her fall.

After several long hours waiting for tests and then results, the doctors could find nothing in the CT scan or x-rays to indicate a concussion or broken bones. It seemed to me that the ER staff thought the visit was precautionary at best, and a nuisance at worst. I suspected that nuisance was their predominant reaction to an elderly, delusional woman with no visible injuries, and I resented their brush-off.

But I was getting used to that feeling and had to shrug off my irritation and focus on the good news. Thankfully, Mom had escaped physical injury…once again. She could go home, without even so much as a recommendation to check in with her own physician. I suspected they were just glad to see us go.

The sunset blazed over the trees lining the hospital parking lot as I walked to my car and pulled up to the portico to retrieve Mom from where she waited in a wheelchair, accompanied by an Emergency Room Attendant. Yes, she could go home. That was good news. What I found disturbing, though, was the puzzle presented by her dizziness, fall, confusion, and visions the past few days. None of the tests had shed any light on that.

Mom was so tired out by the day's ordeal, she asked me to take her back to The DeSoto Beach Club so she could just crawl in bed and sleep.

I promised her I would bring the bag she left at our house over to her place when I came to see her the next day. I also vowed (to myself) I would call Dr. Canada to see if she could help me understand what was happening. Maybe she would expedite an appointment to examine Mom herself since this incident was so unusual. Mom had also asked to go see her ophthalmologist, in case the visual disturbances were related to her Macular Degeneration. That, too, made sense to me.

The many calls and texts exchanged with my sisters and brother to explain the incidents of the past two days gave me confidence that appointments with her doctors were the next step to take.

But...we never got as far as those appointments before another crisis hit.

Mom's Path

Throughout these few days, Mom moved in and out of touch with reality from moment to moment. At times, she seemed perfectly clear-headed, able to talk about her hallucinations as though she wasn't the one having them.

"I know they are not real, Kathy," she'd say. Then she would drift off again, stuck in another fantastical realm she envisioned.

It was an odd combination of rationality mixed with delusion, of a former RN dispassionately assessing her own condition coupled with a terrified, bewildered and even awe-struck, frail woman, working hard to make sense of a world that had taken on so many new emotional qualities.

She wavered, but she hung onto enough rationality to be able to "pass" with the paramedics and medical staff. It was like she was putting on an act for them, hiding what was truly going on so that they would not deem her crazy or delusional, though we both knew she had been in another world on and off for several days.

The most disconcerting aspect to me was that each of these worlds was very real to her while she was in them.

My Path

These were harrowing days. I felt a combination of irritated good humor at Mom's insistence about the "mouse in the house" and deep concern for both her physical and emotional state.

I drew on my Stephen Ministry training to shift my own thinking from dismissiveness to compassion, knowing if I succumbed to the same anxiety she was feeling I could not help her out of the fear. But the fear in her voice triggered something in me, making my past rise up and seize my heart, while at the same time, giving me a strategy to help Mom navigate her anxiety.

It felt like God reopened a door to my own emotions so I could remember and use the lessons of an earlier time. I thought I had put away that era for good. But I was wrong.

I was grateful I could recall enough of the feelings to turn them into action. I was grateful for Jim's presence and calm that night and for God's strength, as this was so disorienting I don't think I would have been able to handle it without leaning on Jim and trusting God to guide me.

Still, I felt a tremendous inadequacy – not so much when Mom was experiencing the anxiety of delusions – I had a strategy for that, but when navigating the medical decisions surrounding all of it. I was just doing the best I could. I didn't even feel at ease calling 9-1-1, for goodness sake!

I needed Jim. I needed my sisters and brother. Jim was at a business meeting the day of the fall, so I was alone with Mom and all that was happening to her. Sure, I could call and talk to any of them, and I did. But unless they saw for themselves, it didn't quite register how disorienting the events of the past two days…no…the past few months had been.

Not only that, I constantly second-guessed myself, because I had not taken her directly to the Emergency Room after she fell. This was the first time I truly recognized the impact the differences in training and profession between my leadership and career counseling background and Lynn's nursing and Peg's social work expertise had on Mom's care. I remember saying to my friend Mary as I recounted the day's events, "Lynn's a nurse, Peg's a social worker…and I am a leadership trainer. Yet, here I am, trying to figure this out. Makes me want to ask God, 'What were you thinking? Why me?'"

By talking this through with Mary, a woman who lived each day depending on God, He gave me an answer, "Why not you? Just lean on me." He brought friends into my life to teach me that lesson.

I was learning the leaning stuff, but I wasn't very good at it yet.

Chapter Ten:
Heartache

It was the following Monday, around 7:45 in the evening, when I got another urgent cell phone call from the staff at The DeSoto Beach Club. My ringer was turned to silent while I participated in a small group class at church, so I didn't pick up the original call. But when class was over at 8:00, and I headed out to the parking lot, I turned on my phone and picked up the message: "Your mom is in Lakewood Ranch Hospital. She called 9-1-1 herself because she was having chest pain. They need you there, Kathy!"

I called The Beach Club immediately while running to my car and then peeled out of the parking lot. *What was going on?!* When I reached the desk attendant, he told me Mom had been at Bingo sitting with Ellen at her usual table when she got up suddenly, making the excuse to Ellen that she was going to use the bathroom. She took the elevator up to her apartment, called 9-1-1, then waited on her couch until they arrived.

Ever a nurse, she knew the intense chest pain she was experiencing meant something grave was occurring. She calmly handled the crisis, as any medical professional would. *Amazing! Foolish she didn't tell anyone, perhaps, but amazing!*

As is the established practice, the emergency crew contacted The DeSoto Beach Club to confirm they were on their way, the first time anyone in charge in the facility knew Mom was in distress. Within minutes, Kim, The DeSoto Beach Club Evening Manager, and her friends Ellen and Agnes were at her apartment waiting with her for the ambulance to arrive. The emergency crew whisked her to the Lakewood Ranch Hospital ER within 15 minutes of her initial call.

On the way to the hospital, I called Jim, then my friends Mary and Nancy, asking them to pray for Mom. Nancy, knowing that Jim was out of town on business and that I would be alone at the hospital, offered to meet me at the ER, while Mary notified our small group leaders to put Mom on the prayer chain. Mom would be covered with God's grace and healing Spirit, that was certain, no matter what was happening to her.

I arrived 15 minutes later. The desk clerk let me right in, the floor nurse leading me down the hall to Mom's curtain-draped cubicle with a serious look on her face. I barely had time to talk with Mom before a radiology tech came to take her for an MRI.

On the way out the doorway, she asked, before succumbing to the pain, moaning softly and closing her eyes, "Kathy, I need a priest. I want the Last Rights. Call a priest for me."

I sat in that empty Emergency Room cubicle, praying desperately for God to heal her. For God to take away her pain. I worried, how would I find a priest to come now? I asked for the Chaplain, but he wasn't Catholic. Mom wanted a priest to give her final absolution and anointing before death, the last of the 7 Catholic Sacraments.

While waiting for Mom to return from the MRI, Nancy arrived. She is my practical, logical friend who can stay grounded in the face of any emergency. She had a plan for finding a priest. She called my former pastor and our friend Elizabeth to let her know that my mom was in the Emergency Room with a serious condition, asking if she would direct us to a priest. Elizabeth knew how to find one. So, with her guidance, I called Our Lady of the Angels and asked for Father Tom.

Within minutes of contacting Elizabeth, one of the aids returned Mom to her cubicle on one of those cold gurneys they use for transport. I snuggled her in with heated blankets offered by the nurse. Then, the doctor walked in to give us the report.

Mom's aorta had dissected, and the separation was growing. I am certain Mom knew what that meant. But to my layperson's ears, the diagnosis wasn't clear at all.

"What is a dissected aorta? And what are the implications of that happening?" I frantically asked.

The doctor explained that the prognosis was as grave as one can be. The aorta, he told us, has two layers in its walls. In Mom's, blood had seeped between the layers and was causing a catastrophic bleed. In some cases, life can be saved by inserting a stent in the aorta, stopping the bleeding and allowing it to heal. But in Mom's case, the tear was in the section between her two carotid arteries, making surgery to implant a stent impossible. Her prognosis depended largely on whether or not the tear spread down the aorta to her heart. If it did, it would be fatal.

The doctor didn't express hope, but instead, encouraged me to call all Mom's loved ones to come to the hospital. He didn't say so, but I later learned that only 5% of those with this condition live without surgery.

Thank God the priest was on his way. Mom was in horrible pain. I was in shock.

Were we going to lose her tonight?

Within a few minutes, Father Tom arrived to hear Mom's confession and perform the Anointing of the Sick. Then, dear friends Elizabeth and Richard, both Presbyterian pastors, arrived. Richard is also a Hospice Physician, so once he learned of Mom's diagnosis he knew how near death she could be.

While Elizabeth, Nancy and I stood talking quietly in the hallway, Richard went to Mom and prayed with her and over her, calling on God's healing Spirit to be with her. We joined in the prayers, trying to comfort her in her pain and fear until the pain meds brought some relief.

Once her pain was under control, she was surprisingly calm. She was fearful of dying without the sacraments, but Father Tom's visit seemed to ease her fear for a while. Richard and Elizabeth's presence and their profound respect for the transition from this life to the next calmed and comforted us all. Her cubicle took on the aura of a chapel, with all of us holding Mom and her spirit up to God.

Reverence and grace filled that space as we sat vigil, waiting… for what, we were not sure.

Waiting

Soon, we learned from the nurses that they would not admit Mom to Lakewood Ranch Hospital, but would be transferring her to a regional hospital, some 15 miles away, because it had a strong cardiac unit that was more equipped to handle her situation. As soon as the medical team could arrange it, an ambulance would take her there.

We waited. And waited. And we waited. And as we waited, my hope for Mom's recovery grew.

Why would they transfer her if there was no hope?

As the hour grew later and later, friends left for home. I called our son, Dave, and asked him to join me in the wait. We hugged, cried and prayed together, and before the ambulance run began, he was able to give Grandma a hug and kiss. Mom had always had a special place in her heart for Dave, so it comforted her to see him. I think it helped them both.

That long night was a blur. On the drive following the ambulance to the second hospital, I was able to contact Jim and Lynn with an updated status. I think Lynn called Peg, Jay and Jill, letting them know what had happened and that we were heading to the Regional Cardiac Specialty Unit. All of them booked flights to Sarasota from their respective homes in Michigan, Indiana, California, and South Carolina, wanting to get there as soon as flight schedules would allow, hoping Mom would hold on.

I was especially grateful that Lynn would be coming soon. As a cardiac nurse herself, she knew what Mom was facing. She could talk with the doctors and give us all the information and explanations we craved. Lynn's flight from Indianapolis was to arrive by noon the next day.

Meanwhile, I'm sure Peg gave the news to Mom's sisters, activating the "Milligan hotline" of all Mom's relatives and friends. Our friends Janet and Neil, who own the condo below us, even offered it to my siblings to stay in while they were in Florida.

Kindness upon kindness and grace upon grace poured over our family like rain.

Once I arrived at the larger hospital and found my way to the Emergency Room from the labyrinth that is their parking garage, it was nearing 1:00 AM, and I had run out of cell battery. Suddenly out of touch with my family, I was fearful. The adrenaline coursing through me heightened all my nerve endings, making me shake; yet my mind and heart worked overtime, desperately trying to offer a steady presence for Mom.

Mom dosed on and off all night, in and out of awareness, while I puzzled about why we remained in the Emergency Room and not in the Cardiac Unit as promised.

When she was awake, I talked softly with her, telling her I loved her and that her kids were all coming. They would be there the next day. We spoke of Heaven, we spoke of Dad and that if God took her home to Heaven, Dad and her own mom and dad and her brother and sisters would be there to meet her. I told her she would not be alone, that I was right here, and that I would be here for her no matter what happened.

Her mother's instinct fierce as ever, her words were of comfort for me, telling me not to worry, that she was strong and not ready to die.

It was 7:30 AM before they moved Mom to a temporary holding room, finally admitting her to the hospital while awaiting a cardiac bed that would allow her the best of care and monitoring. But temporary did not mean substandard. In that temporary room, she received outstanding compassion and care from a male nurse whose name I cannot recall. He smiled and joked and treated her with tenderness, like the precious woman she was, in contrast to the indifference I perceived at the time from the ER staff downstairs.

When I think back upon that night, I realize now that no one expected her to make it through the night. The ER staff didn't have any more information to give me, and they didn't want to admit her – I later learned that Medicare wouldn't pay for a late-night admission if she died before morning. And so, inured to the emotional drama playing out in our tiny, curtained cubicle, the staff monitored Mom's heart rate, pulse, and blood gasses and checked on her from time-to-time. They, too, were in silent vigil. It was just that their expected outcome was light years from what my hopes allowed me to grasp.

At 9:00, a cardiac bed opened up, and Mom was moved to a room right across from the nurses' station, monitors attached, and labs drawn. Once she was settled in, I was allowed to see her. Her energy depleted from the long night's ordeal, she quickly fell asleep. I stole down to the gift shop to pick up a cell charger, and back up to the cardiac floor, missing the surgeon and hospitalist's rounds. *Dang!*

Later, I caught the surgeon charting at a little desk in the hallway. Or should I say, he caught me, bedraggled, exhausted, hopeful but on edge? I distinctly remember rushing back down the hall from calling my sister, Jill, to give her a status report when the surgeon, again a nameless, white coat in my memory, turned to catch my attention.

"Is Mrs. McArthur your mom?" He asked.

"Yes, what do you think of her situation?"

He looked at me, stunned at what I perceived he thought was my nonchalance. He stated, in no uncertain terms, "Your mom is very, very ill. We cannot do surgery. I want you to be sure to call your family to see her. I would do it right away."

For some reason, I flashed a thumbs-up sign, meaning I had already called my family. But that must have seemed inane to him at such serious news.

"Thumbs-up is not appropriate here. Your mom is in a very precarious situation," he said, scolding me, or so it felt when his words fell on my raw nerves. His words, not intended to hurt but to alert me, shot daggers into my heart. Ever since a bad experience with an overworked and testy doctor in the hospital when Dad died, I found myself getting defensive and upset when around what I perceived to be medical arrogance. Kindness and gentleness were called for now, not scolding.

I guess I blew it with that doc. "Hurry up and get here, Lynn" I thought. *Hurry!*

Planning a Goodbye

Before the family arrived, Mom awoke and wanted to talk about arrangements for her funeral. This surprised me, but I listened to her wishes for songs often sung at Mass, and prayers said regularly in Catholic services. I didn't take notes, I confess. I just listened and asked questions where needed.

"I don't want to be buried underground, Kathy. Don't want the bugs to get me."

"OK, Mom, do you want to be cremated?"

To an uninformed observer, it may have seemed macabre, but I hold our conversation sacred. Mom was thinking about the end, even though she said she wasn't ready to die. She wanted plans in place. She didn't want us to have to worry and wonder what her wishes were like we had to do when Dad died.

Jim arrived home late that morning. He met me at the hospital soon thereafter. Lynn came next, swiftly building professional relationships with all on the Cardiac Care floor, easily speaking their language and gathering status updates from doctors and nurses. The rest of the family came in later that day, so Jim and I had a house full, and an overflow 2-bedroom condo to use. *Thank goodness for the favors of friends.*

Mid-afternoon, Jim and I headed home to stock up on groceries for our guests and make sure all was in order for everyone's stay. Lynn and Peg shared the late-evening shift, arriving back at our house by 11:00 or so. Before everyone headed off to bed, Lynn gave us an update, and we worked out that we would rotate into Mom's room in the morning, spending the rest of the time in the waiting room together. If what seemed inevitable happened, no one wanted to be out of touch.

I shared with all of them the conversation I'd had with Mom that day about her funeral wishes and asked everyone to write down anything else she brought up when they were with her.

Loving Words

Rising early the next morning, we carpooled to the hospital to arrive before the Hospitalist's early rounds. Mom had spent the night intermittently sleeping, thinking and somehow coming to terms with impending mortality. Her message to all of us when we arrived, "I am ready to go now. I am at peace. I want to talk with each of you individually."

It was 6:30 Wednesday morning, and something, maybe peace, maybe grace, maybe God's Spirit had touched her soul overnight.

I scarcely remember what she said to me, something about not being too stressed and to take care of myself. I am sure she also thanked me for being there for her these past years. Again, I wish I had written down her words, but the emotion of the moment overwhelmed rational thought.

I know I told her how much I loved her and had felt honored to get to know her better since she'd moved close. I apologized for giving her a hard time when I was a rebellious teen, something that entered my mind from time-to-time when she and I were having fun together, but that I'd never said. I told her how much I admired her strength and courage. And, I hope I reminded her that Heaven would be a glorious place and that she would be welcome there, but I'm not sure I did.

It was a brief conversation, a few sentences, really. It felt to me like she was letting go. She was not fearful anymore. She said that God had comforted her, and she was free. I wondered at the change, at the acceptance, at her care for her kids at this time.

Lynn, Peg, Jill, Jay, and even Jim filed into her room in turn, where she imparted bits of wisdom for each one, specific to their personalities and needs. I don't know what she said to each of my sisters and brother, but Jim told me she thanked him for caring so much for me. That she said I was a shy little girl and that our marriage had enabled me to come out of my shell and thrive as an adult. For this, she was thankful. She thanked him for being such a good son-in-law, for caring for Dad and her during their later years, and that she loved him for it.

I loved her for telling him those things, things Jim only revealed to me as I was writing this when I questioned him about their conversation. Up until this point, he'd held her words closely, keeping her confidence as he'd promised.

Conversations finished, messages delivered, she was ready to go. Still, she hung on, her heart still beating, the aortic dissection not progressing any further.

Would she be one of the 5%? Wouldn't it be ironic, if once she accepted that her death would be on God's time, if that very acceptance turned the tide of her crisis?

From Intensive Care to Rehab

Mom was rallying. By week's end, she was moved to the Med/ Surg floor, no longer considered at death's door, but still too frail and weak to discharge back to her home. To regain her strength after this ordeal, she needed weeks of rehab. We had to find a place for her to go.

Finding a rehab facility – a big job fraught with emotion. Who would say where she could go that would offer the care she needed? Would the hospital make a referral? Did we have to find and select the place ourselves?

We had all just experienced the most difficult of emotional rollercoasters a family can go through. The hospital social worker who conveyed the decision that Mom would be discharged within the week, offered only minimal assistance. Surprisingly, she was in a profession where exceptional communication skills were essential, yet from my perspective, a strong communicator was the last thing I would call her.

The social worker was scarcely available for consultation, overbooked and busy with other patients on the ward who were more trouble, Mom's roommate among them.

The poor soul in the other bed in her room moaned and cried, writhed and tried to get up out of bed, so incoherent that nurses used arm restraints, removed only when they brought her dinner. But no one seemed to have time to help her eat, leaving a tray on her bedside table where she couldn't reach it. A few times, my brother, Jay, noticed her climbing out of bed to move the table closer, posing a fall risk.

I learned something heart-warming about my brother in that situation. He stepped up, spoke gently to her to coax her back to bed, then took the tray and fed her dinner, making conversation so she felt cared for and safe. We never saw anyone else visit her. Jay was the perfect salve for that frightened, elderly woman's worried and addled mind. I smile now as I think of his kindness.

I was so relieved my family was standing all together to walk through Mom's crisis. But after days on end of intense worry, I wasn't feeling so kind. My irritation at the medical bureaucracy had reached its peak. I had to get out of that hospital. I felt that Mom was languishing and that if we had not been there, her care would have mirrored that of her roommate.

Leaving Peg, Lynn, and Jay to work out the rehab arrangements, I called my friend Emily for a walk. I needed to burn off some of this negatively-charged irritation.

Walking with Emily – A Wise Woman's Lesson

As I walked and talked with Emily, she let me vent for a bit.

"The hospital staff on Mom's new floor is falling down on the job. The social worker seems hostile. Nurses let her lay there for days without bathing her or helping her get a shower." Then the big one raised its nasty head, buried deep inside the other complaints and fraught with emotion. "My siblings are taking over. I feel like my ideas don't matter. I know that Lynn and Peg both work in the medical arena, but I don't see how they stand the bureaucracy. I'm the one that Mom relies on. I feel closed out."

When I had let off some steam and wound down enough to hear her, Emily spoke up with her kindly, Kentucky accent, seasoned with her years of coping with life and walking through grief to come out strong on the other side.

"Kathy," she reminded me, "your mom is their mother, too. They care about her as much as you do. Give them some space to do what they do best. You have had your time with her. Step back and let them step up. Let them give to her now."

Oh, I needed to hear that. Yes, I resisted it at first. But as we talked, she gently led me to understand that I was acting in a controlling way that could alienate both my siblings and the medical staff. I may have already done so. I could repair the damage, but I would have to step back and let others take the lead. My protectiveness for Mom's well-being was making the situation worse than it had to be. So was my own discomfort with the uncertainty. It was hard enough to worry about our mother dying. No one needed to fight a turf war, too.

God, forgive me, I thought, as Emily hugged me goodbye. I had no idea I was acting that way.

It's true I am blind to many of my own failings, but He puts people in my path who help me see myself more clearly.

One more layer had just peeled away, exposing my raw core.

Mom's Path

This crisis revealed a side of Mom that had not been evident for a while.

I saw the mom she remained even after all of us were in our 50's and 60's. I saw a compassionate woman seeking to impart final wisdom, all the while assuring everyone she would be alright, despite the fear she naturally felt. And I saw a woman of faith whose belief came to her rescue when facing life's ultimate test, accepting and preparing for one's own death. She did so with dignity, grace and with eloquence and love.

Not many of us get a trial run at that. Mom did, and she passed the test.

My Path

What had this crisis tapped into in me? Where did these feelings come from?

In the circumstances, it was not hard to understand my protectiveness toward Mom. It was hard, however, to understand my righteous indignation and the outright resentment at the medical establishment welling up in me. I am even afraid to write this now, fearing my siblings will take offense at something I am struggling still to understand. After all, Lynn spent close to 40 years and Peg close to 35 in branches of that profession.

But I think I have a few inklings of its origins – my feeling of being out of control; my desperation at not knowing the how and when of the outcome and what to expect; my frustration at not knowing the language surrounding medicine, language that keeps all but the professionals at bay when information is so crucial to processing what is going on; my desire that Mom's end of life be handled with reverence, with spiritual openness and peace, not whirring machines, constant interruptions, hospital food and unruly, desperate roommates; and finally, the hardest to admit, my dismay at being an outsider when I was so used to being the one who made the decisions, who took care of things and made everything alright.

I hated that powerless feeling.

Funny, we are all powerless in the face of death, aren't we?

Well, until I talked with Emily, I was having none of it.

If I am to admit my feelings at the time with complete transparency, I also had a good dose of "How dare they?" and a healthy dose of "Who do they think they are, swooping in here and taking over when I was the one who took day-to-day care of Mom?" self-righteousness. Those were dangerous feelings, feelings that could rend family relationships forever. Feelings that I did not want to own but had to admit were there.

I tried my best to suppress them, but I am sure they came out in my blazing eyes and pursed lips, or worse yet, in my sharp tone of voice – a family trait that more than one of us inherited from Dad.

I knew that it was no one's choice that I lived closest to Mom. I knew that everyone did the best they could to be present for her when their lives and distance allowed.

Whew! What was I going to do with these feelings?

I knew I had to step back, just like Emily advised.

I prayed a lot those few weeks, tried to help by cooking, driving, visiting, trying my best to show appreciation and to get out of the way to allow Lynn and Peg to vet the rehab facilities and find just the right one for Mom. I knew they wanted to help, and they were the best ones for this task. After all, Peg's job was to refer deeply-troubled and ill clients to hospitals or other care facilities. She knew what to look for, knew what was best and how to tell a sales pitch from reality on the care floors.

After much searching, they found a warm, professionally-run facility not too far from my home. Without their knowledge of what to look for, who knows where Mom would have ended up. I am grateful for their knowledge and care in selecting just the right place, one any of us would want for our mother.

I know now, years hence, that the sort of resentment and gut-wrenching emotion I felt are common experiences for care partners. It is easy to think caregiving should go a certain way, to second guess when one is distant and not on the front lines. It is just as easy for a care partner's back to go up in resistance or resentment when suggestions come from those distant but caring souls trying to do their best to be helpful. After all, as Emily said, she is mother to all of us.

What I needed was a walk in my siblings' shoes…seeing the world from their perspective to understand their experience, not just my own.

During the crisis with Mom's dissected aorta, my sight was clouded, and my emotions were raw, blocking my view of anyone else's concerns. I just wasn't the best at looking through someone else's experiential lens, though I knew how to talk the talk and even taught this perspective-taking technique in my conflict management and leadership training classes. It was all well and good in the classroom with adults at work; reality in a live medical crisis was another story for me altogether.

I only hope my short-sighted reactions did not cause permanent damage to my family relationships. I would have to work at that one, too.

I longed to be gentle…but gentleness was still a work in progress.

Chapter 11:
The 5% Woman

M om really was the 5% woman. She beat all the doctors' expectations, surprised us all at her physical resilience, beating all the odds.

What 90-year-old woman survives a dissected aorta, one that is not amenable to surgery, and comes out the other side with her faculties relatively intact?

Mom did.

Once settled into her rehab facility, Mom's recovery was slow but steady. Extended family members arrived to visit, taking time from vacations in Florida to stop by. And it looked like she may be well enough to return home within weeks, depending on how much progress she made regaining her strength and weight lost while languishing in her hospital bed.

Physical therapy was a daily challenge, but she chose to spend much of the rest of the time in her bed. I think she was afraid to put any extra strain on her heart and that unreliable artery by moving around, so to her, bed seemed like the safest place. She moved gingerly, rarely sat when she could lie down and even avoided straining in the bathroom, insisting on enemas or suppositories to move things along.

After the one-week mark in rehab, my siblings all returned to their respective lives in distant states. Jim and I were grateful they rallied to Mom's side during the crisis, but for all of us, home without the additional stress of juggling extended family dynamics was a huge relief.

In the last few days of their stay with us, I know I offended Lynn with a disparaging comment about the medical profession and Mom's nurses…shooting off my mouth in my "speak first engage brain later" habit that I was trying hard to break. I never thought that she would take it as a personal affront to her profession, and therefore a personal attack. In hindsight, that was probably the straw that bent our relationship almost to a breaking point. It would take additional confrontation, the distance of time and the intimacy of long talks late into the night to heal that inadvertent wound.

Day-by-day, Mom was able to navigate the halls with a walker, then showed she could climb a few stairs, eat by herself, stand for a period of time without assistance. Within 3 weeks, she was released back home to The DeSoto Beach Club, newly equipped with a walker, cane, and instructions from the Occupational Therapist to replace her glass dining table with one steadier and one she could more easily notice with her increasing blindness. The therapist also advised us to clear out any obstacles that could pose a fall risk when navigating around her apartment.

Mom agreed to the changes, but the task of making them happen… well…that was my job.

Boost, Snickers and Organic Soup

As Mom settled back into a routine at The DeSoto Beach Club, restrained by self-imposed limits to activity, Jim and I took turns with daily visits. We ramped up the services we employed through Kim's Angel Care, too, because regular timing with her meds was critical to her recovery.

Mom frequently chose to remain in bed all morning, staying in her pajamas the rest of the day. If someone didn't bring her breakfast each day, it might be dinner-time before she ate at all. When I visited, I often found her laying on her loveseat, head on a decorative pillow, still in her PJ's and fuzzy old pink robe. Getting dressed seemed a chore she didn't want to take on.

That she opted for this isolated existence in her small apartment was not under doctors' orders, in fact, quite the contrary. But her latest medical crisis seemed to have zapped her appetite, all her energy, and her motivation. It looked to me that she was experiencing depression, maybe even feeling regret and disappointment that, after all the emotional turmoil she went through getting ready to let go of her Earthly existence, she was still here.

I could coax her to eat, as could Kim, who brought her coffee, with two creamers, toast and soft-boiled egg each day. But the chocolaty drink, Boost, and miniature Snickers bars were the go-to snacks that piqued her taste buds. She went through at least two cases of Boost per week. And, it wasn't uncommon to find empty Snickers wrappers everywhere, including under her pillows. I found myself frequenting Walgreens to pick up a case of Boost and a bag of chocolaty sweets more than was probably good for her – or for me, as I snuck in a few of these chewy goodies every time I visited her.

Chocolate – was that the ticket to recovery from emotional and physical shock? If that's what Mom wanted, that's what Mom got.

I have to admit that this was a time when my own attention wasn't solely focused on Mom's recovery. Our son, Mark, and his fiancée, Terra's wedding was but a few days away. Jim and I, Dave and Jack would all be leaving for Charleston at the end of the week. My sister, Jill, to the rescue, thank goodness!

Of course, Mom's attendance at the wedding was out of the question now. So, rather than join the rest of us in Charleston for the celebration, Jill volunteered to fly in from her home in California to stay at our condo, making daily visits to see Mom to ensure she continued with her recovery regime.

I won't spend a lot of time here discussing the joy of the wedding. That's a story for a different time. But I will say that knowing Jill was on the job caring for Mom offered respite and a sweet balm for our tense and weary souls.

Jill's perspective on health and wellness is that of one who favors locally-grown and raised organic meat and produce. She's a professional Master Gardener working on horticulture programs at local schools, and she's a Massage Therapist who has always put healthy food and exercise high on the list of her personal priorities. Jill tackled Mom's eating issues with her organic vegetable and chicken soup recipes and healthy snacks. Mom responded. By the time we arrived home from that cherished week away to celebrate the wedding, the high point in our immediate family's life, Mom had perked up considerably.

A week with her youngest daughter had restored her body and soul.

Living in Ordinary Time

My own experience as a Presbyterian Elder (yes, this Catholic girl grew up to join Protestant churches) taught me about Ordinary Time, the time in the church calendar between church High Holy Days (I know, I know. That's a Catholic term…). It's the time between Pentecost and when Advent begins the church calendar again, time for focusing on the daily walk in our faith, rather than on celebrating the major holidays.

Well, after Mark and Terra's wedding, we were all living in our own Ordinary Time. Although Mom was less mobile and frailer than before her health crisis, she was with us, often clear-minded, too. I think we all breathed a collective sigh of relief. The frequency of her incidents with random hallucinations and delusions waned, though her prior zest never really returned. She needed a breather from all the physical and emotional strain.

Lynn and I suspected those crazy visions and torments of the spring may have been related to her heart, maybe mini-blood clots reaching her brain. Who knew? Her doctors never said that, but it's the explanation I settled on at the time.

I needed a breather, too, not sure what to expect each day, but relishing a more stable existence. Life seemed to be smoothing out again, thank goodness.

It was a time of healing and slowly growing faith in the future. It was Ordinary Time.

Respite – A Healing Adventure

With Mom stable, I was able to spend more time prepping for our Sister's Hike on the Virginia portion of the Appalachian Trail, stopping by her apartment four or five times per week, but only for a few minutes or an hour or two at a time after a long hike.

With my pack fully-loaded, I alternated each day between practicing the rhythm of hiking poles on the Celery Field hills and just getting used to the weight and the heat by hiking around my neighborhood. All that training paid off in early October when Lynn, Peg, Stacy and I joined up in the Shenandoah Valley of Virginia.

While Jim held down the fort at home, and Kim watched over Mom for her day-to-day needs, I was able to get away and join my sisters on the trip we'd planned at the beginning of the year. We hiked the AT for four days, in driving rain and fog, often the sole hikers on the trail, only to learn on Day Three that we were hiking in the remnants of Hurricane Juaquin as it barreled up the east coast, drowning half of the mid-Atlantic states, including Virginia. No wonder we were almost the only ones out there. We were the only ones foolish and determined enough to brave the winds and lashing rain. *Wasn't that just what we should have expected after the year we'd had?*

It was both the most challenging and the most rewarding physical effort of my life, barring childbirth, of course. I pushed myself to my physical limits, braved peeing in the forest and bear scat (poop to those of you who have never encountered a bear). We faced stinky trail shelters, spiders in our leaky cabin, cold showers at night and the never-ceasing drip of wet, wet, wet. I struggled mightily, up one rugged hillside and down another, one foot in front of the other; planting my poles and pushing onward, sometimes relying on pure grit and my competitive streak to get me through until the next resting spot, not wanting to be left too far behind. If my sisters could do it, so could I. And guess what? We did it!

Not only had we done it, I did it! I could hardly believe I survived hiking that stretch of the AT. I came through that experience stronger physically and mentally than I've ever been. My body now craved daily exercise, and best of all, my relationships with my sisters, so battered during Mom's crisis, healed in the cascade of laughter and fellowship we needed to survive 40 degrees at 4000 feet, and trails too long and steep to accommodate our weary old bones that refused to give up.

I learned how precious family relationships are, and I learned how important it is to take time to heal those relationships and heal myself from the inevitable bruises and stress of caring for a loved one in waning health. I needed that time with my sisters like I needed air. I learned that in order to do a good job caring for someone else, I had to take time to care for myself. Yes, we did it together, and the camaraderie and love that hike gave us would sustain us through the trials to come.

Return to Ordinary Time

Once home to our respective states and families, we began planning for next year's Sisters Hike (scheduled in October 2016 at Zion National Park in Utah), while Jim, Mom and I settled back into a steady routine. The seasons passed, Christmas, Easter, an entire winter and spring in Florida, the best time of the year on the Suncoast.

Mom returned to more activities, sometimes even heading out with her friends on the weekly Beach Club bus trips to Walmart and Publix or Target and Walgreens, picking up little incidentals or just going along for the ride and the companionship.

I did notice she was napping a lot more during the day, often not even rousing if I stopped in to bring her mail up from downstairs, gather her laundry to take home or to tidy her Kleenex-strewn apartment. I learned later that a drippy nose was a notable symptom of her advancing disease, as was losing weight. And she was losing weight, a status confirmed at her regularly-scheduled visits to the cardiologist and Dr. Canada.

Dr. Canada had diagnosed Mom with Diabetes the year before, but now, at 90, she gave implicit permission for all the Boost and candy bars she wanted. Mom continued dropping weight, stabilizing at far less than the 126 pounds she was a year before.

Hmmm? Was something else going on?

Nothing was obvious then, so why invite in worry that hadn't yet arrived? We were still living in Ordinary Time.

Mom's Path

Mom's dementia diagnosis was not yet clear, and rarely, if ever, brought up by doctors as such. From an observer's perspective, she lacked awareness of her compromised thinking and reasoning ability. She dealt only with her physical diagnosis.

Upon arriving home from the rehab facility, she seemed at first to treat physical activity as something that could cause sudden death. It took her several months to regain the physical confidence she had always exhibited before her aorta betrayed her.

As a younger woman she prided herself on her self-care, sometimes taking it to what others might consider extremes. I remember when she and Dad lived in Seattle, while Jay was still a teen, she regularly went to a holistic doctor who performed blood chelation, some sort of procedure in which her blood circulated through a machine to strip out the heavy metals. Those were the days of her regular 5-mile walks and 20 to 30 vitamin bottles on her kitchen counter, taken to boost her energy, her stamina, and her overall health.

With that lifestyle, it must have shocked her that one of her most vital organs put her life at such risk. She must have also been shocked to be one of the few who then survives such a health crisis without life-saving surgery. That awareness put her into a tailspin from which she never really, fully recovered.

She went through the motions of living in ordinary time, but at the same time, seemed less and less sure of herself, relying more and more on me and Jim and her friend Ellen for daily check-ins just to be sure all was still right with the world.

My Path

The summer and fall of 2015 were such a roller coaster ride of emotions and self-awareness that it was hard to take it all in.

We almost lost Mom…but didn't. I almost alienated my sisters…but in the end, didn't. I learned and grew more emotionally than I had in a long time. And within the few days of our Sister's

Hike and all the preparation I did for it, I grew in physical confidence and strength, more than I had ever thought possible.

Milestones were everywhere in those short seasons of upheaval and joy. We celebrated Mom's 90th birthday, and Jim's and my 63rd. Mark and Terra married and we gained a daughter and two new grandchildren. I hiked a chunk of the freakin' Appalachian trail with my sisters…and in a hurricane, no less!

I felt healthier and more fully aware of my capabilities (and my blind spots) than I had bothered to be in the 12 years since my successful breast cancer treatment.

Thanks to the gentle and insightful people in my life, and my growing practice of learning to trust God rather than relying solely on my own plans, and considerable bent to grab for control, I felt closer to our spiritual home than ever before.

I could feel God's presence around me. I sensed His answers and His guidance in real time. I remembered that awe-inspiring feeling of being held by our Creator, feeling it again. I knew He was with me, with Mom, with my family, and as one of my pastors and friend used to say, "All will be well, all will be well. Rejoice always, because you know the outcome."

Ordinary Time was anything but ordinary to me.

Part IV: The Unraveling

Chapter Twelve:
Here We Go Again, Or Do We?

Mom was doing well enough the following spring that I felt comfortable leaving town for a few days to visit my sister, Peg, and then go onto Detroit to meet up with Jim for a visit with Mark and his new family.

We left Mom in Kim's care at The Beach Club, alerting our son, Dave, to be on stand-by for any emergencies. Mary and Nancy also volunteered to keep an eye on her, including visiting her while I was gone. I felt at ease making the trip, knowing she would be just fine with all the safeguards we'd put in place. Aside from increasing lethargy and isolating herself in her room some days, she didn't give us any reason to feel otherwise.

I headed up to Holland, MI on a Wednesday in mid-May 2016. Peg and I went to the Tulip Festival Children's Parade, hiked in Sanctuary Woods and braved the chill of the Lake Michigan winds to take a short walk on the beach. It was fun to see Peg in her element and to visit her darling carriage house across the street from Lake Macatawa, just blocks from the Lake Michigan dunes. And I was excited to drive with her to Detroit, meeting Jim that Friday to attend the opening of the restaurant Mark had been working on for months.

All would be well, right? Well...not quite.

Somehow, while hiking in that idyllic wooded hillside in Holland,

I failed to notice that the woods was posted for ticks. Big signs at the entrance to the trails cautioned all who ventured in to beware of ticks bearing Lyme Disease. I didn't notice the signs then, and I didn't notice the tick that must have bitten me.

I felt fantastic for three days, at my peak in confidence and strength. I remember thinking to myself, "I have become an athlete." Hmm, pride always comes before a fall, right?

By Saturday night, after the grandkids' soccer games, the restaurant grand opening and a rousing family card game with The Cottone's, something hit me like a ton of bricks. I was sick....sicker than sick. I had to go to bed, and I had to go to bed immediately.

I tossed and turned all night, as feverish and achy as I had felt with chemo. No, it was achier than that. If this didn't pass, I would be begging for someone to put me out of my misery. I thought maybe I'd picked up a bug on the airplane – the kind you inevitably get because someone in the seat behind you just can't cover their cough.

I powered through the next day, grateful to be heading home to Florida with Jim on Monday morning. What had hit me took months of doctor visits and tests to figure out and trips to a specialist in Gainesville to confirm. I had contracted Lyme Disease, and it sapped my motivation, my balance, my energy, and my health. But I wasn't able to take time for that diagnosis and subsequent treatment, yet.

We arrived home to another Mom crisis, one that would escalate over weeks, culminating in some very difficult decisions.

Prizefighter

The morning after returning from our short trip, I went straight to Mom's place. I was shocked by her appearance.

Kim explained that she found Mom lying in bed that morning with a huge purple bruise covering a quarter of her face, her left eye swollen shut. Mom confessed to her that she had fallen asleep while watching TV and thought she toppled off her TV stool, hitting her face on the carpeted floor. She must have been knocked out by the unprotected blow, but once she came to, she decided to crawl straight into bed. The comfort of her bed was such a relief after the shock and pain of her fall, she never thought to call anyone for help. So, it was there in her bed that Kim found her in the morning, looking like she'd lost the prizefight of the century.

This time, I wasn't going to take any chances. Off we went to the ER at Lakewood Ranch Hospital again, for x-rays, a CT scan of her head and more hours of waiting for results. She was lucky for the second time and had not suffered a concussion, though, it certainly would not have surprised me if she did.

Only time could heal the bruises she carried. It would take weeks for the deep purple and red bruises to resolve themselves, turning first a lighter purple, then green, and finally showing up as slight shadows across the upper half of her face. They looked so painful. But Mom handled the pain like a trooper, never complaining. It seemed she took this latest incident in stride. What were a few bruises when she'd survived much worse?

On the other hand, I couldn't help thinking that every time I tried to go away, to get out of town, something bad happened. That wasn't exactly true, but it sure felt like it at the moment, especially since I'd felt so rotten myself, barely able to get through a day without a nap; and even then, my joints ached, and I had developed a weird, itchy rash all over my face.

The two of us could have been extras in a horror movie with close-ups that would scare little children.

Sigh! This was not fun.

Keeping Up Appearances

In spite of the setbacks, we tried our best to return to regular routines.

Jim resumed working in his home office, the constant phones ringing and important decisions fueled by daily Starbucks' Americanos with five shots of espresso. I, too, resumed my daily plans. Walks with Nancy or Mary, frequent bike rides or trips to the YMCA, squirreling away time to write for my part-time blogging gig, or do daily chores before running over to Mom's each day for a few minutes or picking up Jack at school a few times per week.

It looked like we had returned to our status quo. For my part, though, I was merely keeping up appearances. I tried to get through each day without falling asleep, itchy rashes and stiff joints aflame as I puzzled over what was going on in my body, along with my doctors...Lyme Disease not yet on the radar.

I kept going, thinking this was just a temporary virus that was hanging on a bit too long. I tried valiantly not to let it stop me.

But then, it happened. Mary and I were about halfway through a 6-mile walk through her neighborhood to check out the newly constructed boulevard and subdivisions nearby. It was around 9:00 in the morning, the late May sun blazing hot, both of us sweaty and eager to get back to her house for some water and a chat in the good old AC. We were just about ready to turn for home when I got a frantic call from Kim.

Here it goes again, I thought, probably another false alarm. But not to Kim. She was more than simply worried. When she came by with Mom's breakfast and to administer her morning pills, Mom had become belligerent. Kim was beside herself, explaining that Mom had thrown her pills at her and threatened her, growling with a crazy-sounding guttural voice, "If you come in here, I am going to kill you!"

Kim was alarmed at Mom's behavior. And so was I. It was so out of character for such a usually mild, pleasant woman. It was as if she were inhabited by an evil spirit or something. *Where was my real mom?*

Kim begged me to come soon because she had to take care of other residents on her morning rounds. She could keep an eye on her for a while, but I needed to come to evaluate the situation myself.

"Of course, I will be there as fast as I can," I said.

Turning to Mary to fill her in, we ran that last 3 miles home to her house – jog/walked and panted for air was more like it. When we got there, we were both sweaty messes, me breathing hard with hair askew and dark sweat stains on the underarms of my shirt and my back. I couldn't go to Mom's like this.

Mary loaned me a sundress and sandals, and I quickly showered in her guest bath, getting ready for the short trip to Mom's. Mary decided to follow me there, in case I needed moral support. We were out the door and on the road fifteen minutes after arriving at her place. I was so glad she had decided to come with me, grateful for her calm presence.

What we encountered was far weirder than anything I had ever experienced with Mom. And I mean REALLY weird…

Red People, Blue People, and You Better Get on the Bus

Mom was sitting up on her love seat, her back stiff and straight, a posture I hadn't seen her hold often. She was still dressed in her PJs and a long, light yellow, cotton robe, her hair sticking up at odd angles. What she said was the thing that set me back.

"Hi, are you one of the red people or blue people?" She greeted me. Then, promptly announced while pointing to Mary, "You're a red person, and you…," she turned and pointed at me, eyes narrowing into a sinister squint, "You're one of the blue people. Blue people are bad. They chop off heads with bands around them," her words slurred, their meaning obscure to us but obviously not to her.

"What are you talking about, Mom?" I asked, startled at her bizarre pronouncements.

She launched into an even more startling soliloquy.

"I am leaving in 10 minutes to go to Viet Nam. I am going to save the city. The red people are good, and they can all come. But you blue people are trying to stop us. We can't let you stop us. The bus is leaving at 5:00, and we have to be on it. If we're not on the bus, we can't be saved. You will not be saved. You're a blue person who chops off heads. Mary, you are a red person. You better get ready;

~143~

the bus is leaving in a few minutes. We have to go because we have to save the city."

When she spotted Kim in the doorway, she rapidly switched into her growling vocalizations. "Tell her to get out of here. If she comes in here, I will kill her. She's trying to keep me here and I have to go save the city."

I stepped briefly out into the hall to get an update from Kim, motioning to Mary to try to keep Mom engaged. Kim confirmed Mom had been raving like this all morning. She had never seen this in her before, nor in any of her other charges. Her behavior was entirely baffling. I assured Kim that Mary and I would try to calm Mom down, but I agreed with her that this really was a medical emergency.

Was she having some sort of stroke? I couldn't take any chances. I would call 9-1-1.

Returning to Mom's living room, I grabbed one of her comfy sweatsuits from her front closet and encouraged her to get dressed, with Mary's help. I told her I was going into the other room to get her toiletries.

Suspicious of my motives, she murmured under her breath, "You blue people are trying to kill us all. You chop off heads."

I locked eyes with Mary who was sitting next to Mom, wide-eyed but steady. Then I picked up my cell phone, walked into her bedroom and closed the bedroom door to speak to the dispatcher on the other end of the line.

The paramedics arrived within 10 minutes. I caught up with them out in the hall just as they got off the elevator with their rolling gurney. I wanted to be sure they knew that although Mom was acting bizarrely, this was new behavior, not her usual self. I also informed them about her fall days earlier and about her dissected aorta 10 months before. Supposedly, it had healed itself, but my fear, which I expressed to them, was that it was leaking or throwing clots, causing her to have weird neurological symptoms. I also told them she was slurring her words. Something was desperately wrong with my mom.

~144~

Paramedics decided they would take her right to the regional stroke center rather than her usual emergency run to Lakewood Ranch Hospital, just in case it was her heart or her aorta or a stroke at the root of this morning's off-the-wall behavior.

As the ambulance pulled out of the parking lot, I sped to the hospital by the only route I knew, down University Parkway to HWY 301 through Sarasota, dialing Jim to fill him in while I drove. He would meet us at the hospital.

I must have beat the ambulance, though I never saw it arrive. The Emergency Room staff had me sit in the waiting room before someone led me to Mom's room 30 minutes later, Jim striding in just in time to join us in Mom's cubicle.

What followed was at times odd, frustrating, hilarious and then infuriating, as I struggled to navigate the mental health emergency system in the state of Florida...

Into the Mental Health Labyrinth

Rather than bring Mom into the usual emergency ward, the paramedics dropped her off in a specialized holding room that can only be described as a cell. Think of a rolling metal garage door leading to a freezing cold, dark grey room, a dingy linoleum floor with only a gurney for her to lay on. There were no windows, no chairs for me or Jim, and nothing at all on the walls. The door to the hallway into the rest of the Emergency Room had a thick glass, half-panel and was locked tight from the outside. There was no way out of this room.

Nurses and technicians came and went by buzzing in, first taking bloodwork, then rolling Mom out for a CT scan to see if she had a stroke or her aorta was springing a leak. I was able to get someone to bring in one chair, but that and a warm blanket for Mom, when she came back from her x-rays, was the extent of the comfort measures offered to her or those of us waiting with her.

Rather than the usual post-test visit by an ER physician, whom I expected would give us the test results, we waited more than 3 hours before anyone came by to give us information.

During that time, Mom prattled on about red people and blue people, turning to me accusingly, "Kathy," she growled," I saw you following that ambulance. You were speeding. You should not have been there. Then you disappeared. I told the ambulance driver that he had to take the red route to the hospital or we would never get there. He did, but you didn't. How did you get here? How did Jim get here?"

I never saw the ambulance while enroot to the hospital, but that didn't matter. Reality to her was her very own reality. And her fantasy continued for hours.

"Let me tell you, Jim", she'd say, "That ambulance needs to be redecorated. It needs a sugar sprule…sprule…," she said, struggling to get the right word. "It needs a…a…a sugar sp…spruce…a sugar spout, so that I can get my sugar. I told the driver that, too. He didn't listen to me, but you should tell him, Jim. They need to redecorate that ambulance. But I fooled them. I hid my pancake. I put it under the cushion so that they couldn't get it. I hid it! HA! They'll never find my pancake."

Jim and I couldn't help exchanging wry smiles at her remarks. If they weren't so tragic, her imaginings would have been hilarious.

Mid-rave, in strode a team of at least five men and women, who declined or simply weren't socially astute enough to introduce themselves to Mom, me and Jim. Mom cried out when she saw them entering, "You can't come in here unless you have red shoes on!"

"They all have red shoes on, Mom," I said, trying to comfort her.

She let them in, as if she had a choice.

After asking her a few questions – the year, her age, the name of our current president – they retreated, leaving us again with no answers and no one to ask.

By this time, Jim's patience was wearing even thinner than mine. He is not one to sit still, waiting for information. Like a flash, he was up and knocking on the locked door to be let out. He was going to find someone to fill us in on what was going on.

Mom caught sight of his retreating back and called out, "Jim, you have a hole in the seat of those pants. You better take them off or get new ones. Give them to that nurse there. She'll take them upstairs, and they will make you a new suit. They make great suits here. Take them off. You can't go around with a hole in your pants!" There was no hole anywhere except in her imagination.

Jim is one who takes great care to look authoritative in any medical encounter, and usually, it works to get him the respect I believe all of us should be offered as a matter of course. He had on dress pants, polished shoes, a sportcoat, and tie that afternoon. Still, the nurse who heard Mom call out to him wasn't swayed. She did not offer any further information, nor did he get any on his foray to the main desk.

This was getting more absurd by the moment. Didn't they care that Mom was nearing 91 and was legally blind, that we had been there for hours and hours and she hadn't had anything to eat all day? We were freezing in that little cell!

What the HELL!!!

Baker Acted – No Way Out!

Around 3:00 that afternoon, Jim had to leave to participate in a conference call for work. I stayed with Mom, who had finally wound down enough to doze on that icy gurney while I sat in that hard, plastic chair, contemplating what could possibly be the reason for the stand-offish and frustrating behavior of the hospital staff. Minutes and then hours continued to tick by.

Suddenly, around 4:00 PM, a uniformed police officer and a woman in a red sweater buzzed in, again neither identifying themselves. "We're taking your mother now," the officer said.

"What?! Where are you taking her? What's going on?" I asked, every part of my body sounding off alarm bells.

I got no answer from the officer, nor from the red sweater woman.

He rolled Mom out of the room, down the hall and apparently across the busy street to another facility. I tried to follow but was stopped by "Red Sweater" who finally identified herself as the hospital social worker.

"Come into my office," she said.

Of course, I followed her, full of urgent questions and hot indignation. "Where are they taking my mom?"

"Your mom has been Baker Acted," she stated coldly. "We have a court order to admit her to the psych ward across the street. You can see her tomorrow. Here is a number you can call to get more information," she said, with no emotion whatsoever, handing me a bent and soiled card with a phone number printed on the front before turning her back on me.

"Wait. What? What is Baker Acted? And what is the psych ward? I need to know what is happening to Mom. I have her Power of Attorney and Medical Power of Attorney right here. I'm responsible for her wellbeing. Tell me what's going on here!"

But my plaintive questions fell on deaf ears. "I cannot tell you more due to privacy issues," she said as she ushered me out the door.

Note: I learned later that the Florida law – The Baker Act – allowed authorities to petition a judge to order a person into a psychiatric facility for three days, without recourse, if they are deemed a danger to themselves or others. No input from family, no arguing with the decision. A judge's order...and off they go. The horror of the potential impacts of a mental illness and the havoc it can wreak on all involved led to this law, but it is little understood by most of us until a loved one is caught up in the impenetrable process. And Mom was one of those people.

The Psych Hospital, Anything but a Tranquil Seaside Resort

Within minutes, I was crossing that same busy street they'd rolled Mom across, walking into the sole public access door to the Regional Psych Ward.

The ward was in a self-contained, fortified building, with thick glass panels separating the chairs (set out for visitors) from the reception desk and office staff behind them, when anyone actually manned the desks and empty chairs in that office, that is.

I punched the buzzer to let someone know I was there. It took a full 20 minutes before a young woman appeared. "May I help you?" she asked through the intercom phone.

I explained what had happened and that I was frantically trying to get more information about my mom who apparently had been transported to this facility thirty minutes ago. "I need to see her," I said, "I need to know that she is alright. She is blind with Macular Degeneration, hard of hearing and is nearly 91-years-old. Unless someone she knows is with her, she'll be frightened out of her mind here. Can you help me? I have her Power of Attorney and Medical Power of Attorney with me if that's what you need. I have to get to her."

The young woman shook her head, "I'm sorry, she is being evaluated now. I cannot tell you anything more. Your mom will be here for at least 3 days, by court order. Your Power of Attorney will not do any good in this case. But I can copy them for our files, if you like."

Numb and madder than Hell, I handed the papers through the slot in the glass barrier while saying, "I need to know more about what is happening to my mom, and I need to tell someone about her medical history. She is in no shape today to fill anyone in on her history. Don't you need her medical history, for God's sake?! She had a dissected aorta ten months ago. She fell a few days ago and has bruises on her face. Is there anyone in authority I can talk to? This is absurd!"

My agitation rose to a level that was not going to do my case any good. So while she copied my legal documents, I stepped away and took a few deep breaths, then tried another tactic.

"Look," I said, "I understand that with the HIPPA laws in effect, you feel you cannot tell me anything, in spite of what I believe is my legal right to know, as evidenced by the documents you just copied. But can I at least talk with someone to tell them about Mom, to share information about her so that the medical staff has the full picture? She is in no shape to speak for herself, and I am worried that her heart or her aorta are causing this episode. No one in Emergency would tell us anything, nor did they ask me about important history issues that they should know to treat her appropriately." I tried to speak as calmly and as professionally as I could, hoping to win her acquiescence.

No dice.

"Let me take your name and number, and I will have Sarah, the Social Work Intake Coordinator, give you a call. This is Memorial Day weekend, you know, so we have a short staff on this evening. Visiting hour is not until 1:00 to 2:00 tomorrow afternoon, and no one is available for you to speak with now. If you want to see your mom, you'll have to come back at visiting hour," she stated firmly, handing me a paper with the rules and strictly enforced times for visits at the psych ward.

You'll just have to come back," she said, "…after your mom has gone through intake and is settled into her room. You'll be able to see her tomorrow." With that, she turned and walked away.

I was left standing in the lobby of that dingy, locked building, the steam of extreme frustration visibly rising off my brain.

Visits to the Dark Side

I drove home defeated, knowing I had to bring my siblings up to speed, and that I had to figure out the rules of the system that Mom had fallen into, all because I dialed 9-1-1 that morning, based on what I perceived to be a dangerous health crisis.

From the disposition of her situation, it was obvious that the doctors didn't think that a stroke or her dissected aorta were the issues that morning, but that her mental state definitely was. Of course, they didn't know Mom. And they certainly didn't say that they were considering possible dementia.

They ignored my pleas to speak for her. But they hadn't been through the squirrels, the pink trees and the floating ties with her like I had. They only had their one day of observation to go on, and my word, which in this case, wasn't something they were interested in hearing.

After talking with Lynn, Peg, Jill, and Jay, Lynn volunteered to call the Intake Coordinator to see if she could get more information. She was no more successful than I was with the team on-call that night.

By morning, however, Sarah (the Coordinator) reached me on my cell phone so that I was able to tell her all about Mom. She also spoke with Lynn, filling her in on the Intake Interview and telling her that Mom didn't seem delusional to her, at all.

The thing is, Mom answered all her questions, but she gave them off-the-wall answers, information that was nowhere near true, but that seemed true to someone who didn't know her. For example, she told Sarah she'd lived in Florida for twenty years, first in Ft. Lauderdale then in Daytona, before coming to Sarasota ten years ago. *All untrue.* She said she was a nurse and that she had two daughters. *What happened to the other three kids?* Again, partially true, but not accurate.

Had the staff taken the time and care to ask me about her situation, I could have filled them in on everything they needed or wanted to know. *But no.* Sarah said that unless I had Guardianship for Mom, no one could talk with me. (Apparently also untrue, I later learned in a consultation with an Elder Attorney.)

For God's Sake! What a stupid system, I thought. This is unconscionable, and if I have a chance, my Representatives in Tallahassee will definitely hear about this and so will the Hospital Administrator. I was fuming! I was HORRIFIED!

But, dutifully, I drove back that afternoon, Saturday, arriving promptly fifteen minutes before Visiting Hour began so I could queue up with the other visitors.

The rules for visitors said that we had to leave all belongings in the car, bringing into the facility only a car key. As we waited to be wand-ed by a security guard, then let in one-by-one to see our respective "inmates", I observed the others in line.

It's hard to judge by appearances, but I bet they felt like I did… like we were entering a prison, not a hospital. I'm sure the rules were there to protect patients from harm and to keep contraband away from the addicts there seeking treatment, still…it felt very uncomfortable to have this sort of security for a woman in Mom's state of mind and tiny physical stature.

Mom was shaken by her surroundings, but very glad to see me. "Get me out of here, Kathy," she begged quietly as if afraid someone might hear her. "This is a psych hospital. I don't need to be in a psych hospital!"

She remembered nothing of the day before, her raving about red and blue people and threatening to kill Kim if she set foot in her apartment. But she did have full grasp of her faculties now. Her mind had cleared of all delusion. She recounted how she had been put in a room with two, 20-something girls, both with deep depression, one with substance abuse issues who kept creeping up to her at night, stealing her only blanket. She expressed concern for those girls But of course, she knew she didn't belong in that environment herself.

And Mom was right. *Who in their right mind would professionally judge it appropriate to place a 91-year-old, frail, blind woman in a room with two mentally ill young girls?* There was no way she belonged in this setting. *What were they thinking to bring her here?* If what she really needed was psychiatric care, wasn't there a geriatric psych ward somewhere in the surrounding area?

"I'm behaving, Kathy," she whispered. "I know what I have to do to get out of here. I am acting completely normal. They think I am crazy, but I am not crazy. If I toe the line, I can get out of here quicker. I did my psych rotations in nursing school, remember?"

"You're right, Mom," I said, trying my best to comfort her. "Keep on doing what you're doing. Jim and I are working to get you home as soon as we can."

The hour passed quickly, and I promised to come back the next day at 1:00. As I turned to walk away, following the staffer down the hall, Mom gave me a little wave. I choked back the tears, sadness, and rage competing in my head. I tried to wrap my mind around what was happening, hating that it happened on my watch. I felt responsible. After all, I was the one who chose to call 9-1-1. Never again, I vowed. Never again.

Sunday's visit, with Jim and I both checking in on Mom, yielded similar results, only this time, she had stories of how the staff made her attend a group therapy session to process her feelings. She recounted how the young person sitting across from her at breakfast had gotten angry and shoved the table at her, jamming her in the ribs. *Where were the staff when this sort of thing happened to an elderly woman? I had to get her out of there, and soon.*

Despite our efforts, we were powerless until the three days had passed.

Escape from Alcatraz

By Sunday evening, two full days and two nights with Mom in the facility, we finally got the name of the attending psychiatrist. I left word with his answering service that I wanted to speak with him as soon as possible, hoping to receive a call that evening.

It wasn't until 11:00 Tuesday morning that I finally heard from him.

I was just getting into my car at the grocery store when he reached me on my cell. He had been away for the Memorial Day weekend and had just completed reviewing Mom's file, pronouncing her diagnosis with conviction over a single phone call. "Your mom had psychotic delusions. Diagnosis…Dementia of Alzheimer's type. She needs 24/7 psychiatric care. She should not go home until you find somewhere for her where she will have round the clock access to a psychiatrist. I believe she is in the best place for her. I advise you to leave her with us until you find another similar place for her. Our staff can give you recommendations on where to check. I don't advise you to take her home at this time."

Keep her there? I don't think so. Not if I can help it.

"Sir," I replied. "My mom is nearly 91, she is frail, blind and hard of hearing, and they had her in a room with two young women who were not kind to her. She was shoved at breakfast and made to go to group therapy to process her feelings when she can't even see. If she needed psychiatric care, she should have been in a geriatric psych ward, not the situation in which she finds herself now. Now, you say she has dementia, and I don't doubt that. But dementia is not a mental illness, is it? I thought it was a brain disease," I countered. "This makes no sense to me. I am not going to keep her there. I think it's dangerous for her. She was scared and alone. No one would talk with me, even though I have Medical Power of Attorney, and your staff didn't watch out for her as they should have. I am very unhappy with how she's been treated. I know a place that has a 24-hour, on-call psychiatric nurse practitioner and may be able to get her a room there. But in any case, I will be picking her up today, as soon as possible. Please sign her discharge orders. I will be there by 1:00."

"Okay, but you are taking her home against my recommendation," he replied. "When you check her out, the staff will provide you with further resources. Good day!"

He sure didn't like me talking back to him, giving him frank feedback about the facility under his charge. But at that point, who cared? That was it. Mom was sprung.

Now, I had to scramble to find her a place to go…

She could not return long-term to The DeSoto Beach Club because they did not have assistance available after 8 PM at night through early morning hours. Sure, I could hire Kim's Angel Care to provide an overnight staffer, but the cost for overnight hours would be prohibitive. And, after the latest incident, The Beach Club management may be reluctant to have her stay there. *What other options were there?*

Before I figured it all out, I called Kim to make sure she and her staff would continue to be there for Mom during the day, at least until I found another spot for her. Kim agreed, relieved that Mom had returned to her normal self. Mom was one of her favorite people, and to see her in such a state was upsetting to everyone. Kim, Ellen, and all Mom's friends were happy she was coming home. For the time being, they would keep an eye on her.

I took Mom home to The Beach Club that afternoon, both of us relieved and worn out by the ordeal. She went right to bed. Me? I went home and called the Assisted Living (AL) facility I knew about in Lakewood Ranch. I had to get Mom into AL with 24/7 access to a psych professional, and I had to do it quickly before she had another delusional episode.

Goodbye, DeSoto Beach Club. You were perfect for a season. But the season was changing. Mom had to move on.

Mom's Path

Psychotic Delusions – Dementia of Alzheimer's Type.

We didn't tell Mom her diagnosis. And we still haven't.

In fact, it has changed several times since then, depending on her behavior at the time and who is doing the diagnosing. Temporal Lobe Dementia. Lewy Body Dementia. Alzheimer's. At this point, what difference does it make what it's called? It only matters that she has the care she needs.

Why tell her? Why make things worse than they already are?

To us, any kind of dementia was a tough diagnosis to accept. We still suspected some sort of oxygen deprivation or stroke, rather than pure dementia. And heck, it could be any of the more than 100 types of dementia. How would we ever know for sure?

From Mom's perspective, she was perfectly fine, no longer remembering the delusional periods after her consciousness returned to its normal state. When she was delusional, she insisted her worldview was the only correct one, yet when she was clear-headed, the delusions never happened. She viewed that stint in a psych hospital as a huge mistake.

She didn't think she needed to move away from The DeSoto Beach Club, either. She hated to move for many legitimate reasons – her friendships at The Beach Club, her familiarity with Kim, with the physical layout of the facility, with her apartment and where everything was stored. Moving posed a dramatic shift in all those things. And just the thought of it brought on resistance, sadness, and fear.

Changing one's dwelling place after years is traumatic for anyone. Changing it at 91, with encroaching blindness and dementia, is devastating. Yet, she heard the doctor say she needed someone there for her 24 hours per day, not just during the daylight and early evening hours. She was adamant she didn't want to live with her kids, and the doctor said she absolutely should not live anywhere without available psychiatric care.

We had a dilemma on our hands.

I promised I would find her somewhere nice and that she had the right to refuse any place she didn't like, so she reluctantly acquiesced.

But it hurt. It hurt a lot. She was losing her home and her friends...again. How would she ever adapt to a new place?

This is a cruel disease, for sure...no matter what you call it.

My Path

During the entire month of June, I felt like I could hardly breathe – the stress, worry, my own Lyme Disease and the emotion of coping with Mom's decomposition were so heavy.

I had failed to protect her from a Florida Law – The Baker Act – which requires a Judge's order to place someone in psychiatric care for a period of 3 days if they cannot speak for themselves and are considered a danger to themselves or others.

How could I fail when dialing 9-1-1…a call that was supposed to protect your loved ones in an emergency?

Yet, that's what happened. I was there to speak for her, but my input was ignored. I didn't know enough about the mental health laws in our state. And I quickly found out that even my Medical Power of Attorney couldn't save her from a Judge's order. Once a Judge rules, that's it…for 3 days.

The law makes sense for those who really are mentally ill or suicidal, who are a danger to themselves or others. I understand that. It may have made sense for Mom…IF…there had been a geriatric psych ward with experts in dementia available. But in this case, Mom's family was frozen out of the decision loop, legal documents giving us the rights to make decisions on her behalf in hand or not.

It just occurred to me while writing this that perhaps the hospital staff took one look at Mom's face, where she had those big (but waning) bruises and thought perhaps her family had abused her. I am horrified by the idea they may have thought the worst – not that anyone insinuated it during the ordeal. But why else did they keep Jim and me so completely shut out of the process? Was it really HIPPA Law privacy concerns?

Was this all normal?

If it was, it shouldn't be.

Powerless was not a feeling I liked. I was used to taking care of things. But not this time. Powerless in the face of Judicial Power…that was me. And I didn't wear it well.

Chapter Thirteen:
Practicalities and Prayer – Finding Mom a New Home

I t's funny how things fall into place – and as a result, I have stopped thinking in terms of coincidence and started thinking of Divine Grace. Here's one of the reasons why...

A few months before Mom's incident with the red people saving the city in Viet Nam, my friend Susan asked me to tour a new assisted living/memory care facility with her, just to check it out. I didn't think we would need a place like that. After all, Mom had been doing okay that spring. But I wanted to support my friend.

Susan's husband had Alzheimer's disease and still lived at home. She needed to see if the facility in question would be a good place for him...eventually...so, we decided to make an appointment for lunch and a program that was offered via a mailer.

The brand new facility was spotless, light and airy. It was only partially full, so they were courting new residents with move-in assistance and special rates. It was similar to many other facilities in town, but only six miles from our condo by back roads, the closest to us by far. There'd be no need to take the highway to get to Mom anymore. The food was excellent, the rooms spacious and bright and the staff accommodating.

They explained that all staff had to go through "Positive Approach to Care" training, an approach to dementia care created and developed by a wonderful woman named Teepa Snow. *(More about that in the Appendix.)*

Best of all, they had an arrangement with a Psychiatric Nurse Practitioner who was the one giving the after-lunch presentation. I liked her a lot. She assessed each resident as they moved in, then, as needed, she prescribed and monitored medications in consultation with a Geriatric Internal Medicine Physician. They both made house calls on a weekly basis.

At the time, Susan judged the facility too new, the food not to her liking, and her husband not ready for such a move. I chalked it up to research and a free lunch and moved on. I never thought it would be our family who would require such a place so soon. But when challenged by that psychiatrist to find somewhere for Mom immediately, I knew I had just the right facility – Inspired Living at Lakewood Ranch.

When I called, they were able to reserve a room for Mom to move in within a week or two, if we could get it together to make it happen.

They arranged for us to come by to give Mom a tour and would help with the long-term care insurance papers I needed them to sign in order to activate her insurance – an essential step if we were going to afford the increase in fees over the rent at her Independent Living Facility.

Mom liked the room she picked out and enjoyed the food in the dining room and the staff who greeted her and showed her around. It seemed like everything was falling into place. At least, in advance of the move, I had her agreement that her new home would be a suitable spot for her.

Who knew that this part, at least, had all been worked out in advance. God's funny like that. He takes care of things…if you listen…and if you let Him.

Moving's No Cakewalk

I don't want to mislead anyone into thinking this was a cakewalk. It wasn't. Not At All.

I had to make sure Mom's recovery from her episode was carefully monitored, meaning Kim, Jim and I took turns each day checking in on her and making sure Dr. Canada had a chance to examine her after she returned home from her stay at the psych ward.

Oh, and I had to contend with negotiating our way out of The Desoto Beach Club rental contract. There were financial issues to sort out with her long-term care insurance company and my siblings, movers to arrange, her household goods to sort through before packing up, medical records to copy and send to insurance, long-term care and new residential contracts to copy, sign, overnight mail and fax *(Who faxes anymore, anyway?)* Paperwork, paperwork, paperwork.

I was drowning in administrivia. And, unfortunately, I was still sick as a dog with as yet undiagnosed Lyme Disease. Break out the violins, right? This was too important to put off. Period. Mom needed me and Jim, Dave and anyone else we could muster. It was all hands on deck.

Siblings – The Challenge of Caring from a Distance

Most importantly, I needed to include my sisters and brother in this critical decision process. (I had learned that lesson from Emily on one of our walks, remember?) But this item was the most difficult of all to muddle through.

Not everyone in my sibling department was in complete agreement, at first. The positive concern for Mom was shaded by undercurrents, ripples of doubt about the diagnosis, the necessity of a move, the speed with which I was making this happen, and on and on. Over the ensuing days, one sibling or another put on the emotional brakes, each speaking with Mom's best interests at heart, but not wanting to do the wrong thing by her. No one absolutely put a foot down, stopping forward progress, but it was evident on our calls that making the decision on moving at this fast pace caused some of my siblings a lot of angst. And they couldn't help but feel that way.

Every one of us wanted the best situation for Mom's happiness, safety and care. But no one else in the rest of the family had witnessed her psychotic ramblings, nor heard the ominous warning delivered that Tuesday morning by the psychiatrist. It was hard for them to simply take my word regarding events so drastic and so extreme. Their incredulity was easy to understand.

Still, urgency dictated we had to do something…and soon.

Sometimes, you just have to act.

Facing her questions head-on, Lynn decided to fly down to assess the situation for herself and to help with the move. Thank goodness for her flexible job and the Family Medical Leave she had put in place while Mom was in the hospital with her aorta. She could take a few days to stay with us, helping with all the logistics, while forming her own opinion about Mom's circumstances. Organization was Lynn's strong suit, and it was a welcome relief to have another set of hands to dig into all that needed to be done.

Before she arrived, Jim reached out to a friend who was a geriatric/ elder attorney specializing in cases like ours. She's a crackerjack lawyer when it comes to Florida Elder Law. When I consulted with her, she informed me that the hospital staff was wrong for freezing us out of information, ignoring my Medical Power of Attorney. Guardianship, however, was not called for by law and not necessary in our case, no matter what the staff at the psych hospital said. The elder attorney advised against it. It was expensive and may have complicated the care decisions I had to make by adding decision-making layers we really didn't need. She did encourage me though, to proceed with moving Mom into the new assisted living facility. I was responsible for her well-being. After the weekend in the pysch ward, that was the only rational choice.

I would definitely share this advice with Lynn when she arrived.

Clash of the Titans? **Better Choice - Phone a Friend**

I didn't know until months later what had set Lynn's and my nerves on fire the week she stayed with us. At the time, I couldn't figure it out, but tension was bubbling hot under the surface.

Maybe Lynn wished this crisis had not happened when she was so far away, wanting to weigh in sooner. Perhaps it was the inconvenience of traveling to Sarasota a few days early when she had planned to vacation on our beaches with her husband the following week. Perhaps it was the close quarters and the workload needed to make Mom's move happen. Maybe I got into one of my directive moods again. Maybe my aching joints made me testy. Maybe I was sick of second guessing myself and decided to stand for Mom my way, no matter what anyone else thought. Maybe we were just both stressed and tired.

I don't know. But what I do know is that a silly fight over where to donate extra furniture and household goods almost fractured my vital, cherished relationship with my sister. Yes, sparks were flying, eyes flashing and the phone line to our sister Peg, the social worker, burned with our frustrations.

What spilled out of us, I am afraid to say, were accusations about how unreasonable I was, or she was, or the situation was. Peg sure got an earful from both of us that week. But with her calm, great-listener approach and our determination, we got through it, forging an uneasy truce.

It was only when Peg maneuvered the sleeping arrangements on our next Sister Hike to Zion National Park that October that we were able to resolve it fully. By Peg's design, she, Jill and Stacy would share one room and bath while, Lynn and I shared a bath, bedroom, and a king-sized bed for the week. On that trip, we kept our distance at first, me still nursing Lyme Disease and by doctor's orders able to hike only every day, while Lynn and the others took off for some challenging scenic adventures.

But in the enchantment of the environment, way up in the high desert where the Milky Way glowed at night and the sparkling eyes of scores of mule deer haunted the still moonlit pre-dawn, we found our footing again. As we lay there chatting in the dark, out came our hurts, our hopes, our fears, and our forgiveness, mixed with doses of regret, humor and the awe of a place so beautiful it seared our hearts with its images.

Siblings…God's wise and wonderful arrangement to give us solace and keep us in check. We are so lucky to have each other – frustrations and all.

Mom's Path

While her daughters and the rest of the family worked behind the scenes, struggling to orchestrate a smooth transition, Mom fretted about the upcoming move.

She didn't want to give up her important personal belongings, she wanted all her clothes, even if she had not worn them for years. Although she had just experienced a severe psychotic episode, she remained clear and in touch with reality during the interim time before the move.

Who could blame her for wanting to preserve as much of her life as possible, as was comfortable and comforting, when all her internal markers of her identity were fraying?

Lynn was able to ease her discomfort by working on the external, the tangible evidence of normalcy. With Mom, she carefully planned the layout for her new studio apartment, helping her select pieces of furniture that would easily fit the design. To counter the feelings of loss that came with giving up items of clothing that represented earlier, happy times to her, clothes that simply would not fit in her more restricted closet space, I offered to store her out-of-season garments at our condo so she could have them when she needed them, setting her mind at ease, at least a little bit.

Mom promised her friends she would visit often and that they could come over any time, something that with their restricted mobility would require as much pre-planning as an international summit to pull off. I agreed to make it happen, though I wasn't sure how.

Moving day was coming at her like a freight train. But she acquiesced. She trusted us to do right by her. She covered her fears with cooperation, though that was not her usual habit when she was unsure. Rather than her feisty self that rose up during times of dramatic change, this time she retreated into a more timid persona.

The last few weeks took an enormous toll on her personality. I think she sensed that the speeding train of determination barreling down the tracks toward her next season of life was unstoppable, whether she agreed or not.

Pausing for a moment to imagine the fear she must have felt seizes my heart, nearly stopping it cold.

My Path

Wow! Lynn and I were silently sparring with one another in ways neither of us would if we weren't close family members, sisters only 17 months apart in age. *What was this about?*

In mulling it over after the dust settled, I realized that raw sibling stuff from childhood can rise again to greet you, smacking you in the face when encountering crises together long into adulthood. The dynamics of family order and place, evident while growing up, no longer fit when interacting with our fully-integrated adult personalities. Yet, they persisted, rising out of the deep lagoon of our subconscious to bite us.

Navigating these fraught emotional landscapes takes conscious effort, examining, and trying to understand the perspective of the other, even when it is not what feels good. It takes prayer and forgiveness – the Divine Grace to "act as if" until our spirits get the message.

Family matters more than our individual needs. We are all on the same journey. It is much easier when we travel it as one.

I know that now. But it took a few dark moments to figure it out.

Chapter Fourteen:
Living an Inspired Life

The Psychiatric Nurse Practitioner and staff at Inspired Living advised me that the best thing for Mom was to help her settle in, then give her a week (or even two to three weeks) before resuming regular visits. This would give her time to establish a relationship with her new caregivers and become conditioned to her new surroundings.

So, that is what we planned. We'd get her settled in, fixing up her place to reflect the familiar as much as possible, then retreat, allowing the staff to guide her and orient her to her new home.

It was hard advice to take, but we had to learn many difficult-to-navigate new ways of interacting with Mom from those who were skilled and practiced in dealing with individuals with the disease of dementia.

This was a new path…one we hadn't walked before.

Moving Day

Moving day was a well-orchestrated, three-dimensional chess game.

No one wanted Mom to witness the dismantling of her current home. So, Jim picked her up as usual, taking her for a ride in his sporty convertible. That morning, she never looked back, seeming to forget she wasn't going back to The DeSoto Beach Club. Jim's job was to keep her occupied and happy while the rest of us handled the move's logistics.

Jim said he got the best part of the deal, and I agree he was the best one for the job. Mom loved Jim and trusted him completely. In his care back in our condo, she could doze in her favorite chair or in the guest room, chat and laugh with him, and eat lots and lots of chocolate ice cream which he had a habit of offering her anytime she visited us.

I took The DeSoto Beach Club duty, guiding the movers – helping interpret our sorting and labeling process so that they could load Mom's goods into the truck in the right order. What boxes went to our place? Which pieces of furniture went to Inspired Living? Finally, which pieces were to be donated? Those designated as cast-offs would either go to Goodwill or the movers would find another way to dispose of them. (At this point, I had stopped caring about that little detail. An old chair or table just weren't worth the conflict they could cause.)

The guys we hired at the advice of Inspired Living's Move-In Coordinator were prompt, capable and efficient. By 1:00 in the afternoon, her apartment (her home for the last 4 ½ years) stood empty. I offered Subway sandwiches and my thanks to the movers, said my goodbyes to Kim, stopped in the office to turn in the keys and pay the prorated rent. I circled back to Mom's table in the dining room to touch base with Ellen and Agnes, inviting them over in a few weeks to Mom's new digs for a small birthday celebration for her 91st year. Then finally, I was done. I turned and walked out the sliding glass doors for the last time. Yes, goodbye, Desoto Beach Club. We will all miss you and the memories forged with friends here.

That day, just like Mom, I never looked back.

Meanwhile, at Mom's new home at Inspired Living, Lynn and her husband Lowen, who had just arrived to help before their vacation, were already hard at work. They placed furniture as it arrived on dolly after dolly, up the elevator and down the long hall to Mom's new studio apartment. They hung clothes in the closet and pictures on the walls, making her room look and feel as close to what she was used to as possible. For a much smaller space, it really felt like home.

All of us joined her for dinner that night, promising to return in a few weeks for a 91st birthday party in the alcove of the Inspired Living dining room.

Bye for Now, Mom

We left that evening hopeful, but with trepidation.

We knew that Mom would be well cared for, as the staff had proven strategies for integrating a new resident into new surroundings. But her sight issues and her intermittent delusions worried me…worried all of us. Still, we wanted to give her a chance to become familiar with her new home and with the new caregivers on her floor.

So we stayed away, with me simply calling the staff daily to get updates on her progress settling in.

All seemed well.

House on Fire! Get Me Out!!!

Then, one night about five nights after move-in day, the positive reports changed.

Mom had awoken in the late hours before midnight, terribly frightened by a dream or vivid delusion. The staff heard her screaming and pounding on the window, in a fearful panic that the building was on fire and that she would burn to death, unable to find her way out of her room or the building.

We never knew what sparked that terror, but it took the staff all night to help her calm down and go to sleep. They called me the next morning, asking me to stop by to reassure her that she was safe and that she wasn't alone. I reminded her that the nurses' station was just one door down from her room and that they would check on her periodically during the night. Nothing could hurt her here. Reluctantly, she accepted my reassurances.

Knowing this was a difficult transition for her, I decided to accompany her to the dining room and look around for another woman who was alone and who seemed friendly and may want a new dining partner. Connie, with her sweet 94-year-old smile, welcomed Mom and me warmly to her table by the door.

From that meal on, Mom and Connie's friendship grew. They took their noon and evening meals together and often sat outside in the rocking chairs on the lanai in the evenings, just chatting and getting some air. And, when a room opened-up on the Third Floor, right next to Connie's room, one that was less expensive than Mom's, we made arrangements for the two of them to live next door to each other.

The immediate crisis was averted. Things were looking up at Inspired Living.

Party Like It's 1955

We held that 91st Birthday Celebration for Mom in the dining room alcove at Inspired Living three weeks after she moved in. Yes, the celebration was in a congregate dining room, but you would have thought we were in the finest restaurant in town. The Chef came out to greet us, to offer us a preview of the menu, filet or chicken with twice baked potatoes and haricots vert. And, of course, a specialty dessert. After the main course was cleared away, the entire staff circled our table, singing Happy Birthday to Mom along with Ellen and Agnes from The Beach Club, Connie, and Jim, David, Jack and I, as she blew out the candles. It may not have been the family party of a year ago, but it delighted her, all the same.

Group activities at Inspired Living included family members as much as possible. They hosted a Halloween party for grands and great-grands in which we all dressed in costume; the kids bobbing for apples and Trick-or-Treating from wheelchair to walker in the expansive lobby and dining room. Easter brunches featured the Easter Bunny for the kids and a lobster and steak buffet that welcomed as many family members as one cared to invite. St. Patrick's Day brought out the green beer and Irish musicians, and every Wednesday was Wined Down Wednesday, a favorite of Connie's and Mom's.

One Wednesday, I stopped by just in time to catch the weekly celebration. As I stood in the archway to the dining room listening to the salsa band that had set up in the corner, there came Mom, partying like the celebration was hers alone. I spotted her in the crowd as she hopped up from her chair and grabbed her walker with more agility than I had seen in a long time. Then…she started dancing…conga-line, no less! Her tiny self, leading a conga line throughout the dining room. Step, Step, Step, Kick, hips swaying to the music, hands clapping and swaying in the air. It was hilarious and heartwarming.

We all had to join in, weaving and hopping throughout the tables, staff, guests and residents alike, laughing and high-kicking until we were all out of breath. This place suited her. Watching her dance – dancing with her – was a joy I'll never forget.

And…the staff at Inspired Living really did up Christmas in a way that suited Mom's holiday sensibilities. They held a door decorating contest and open house, and Mom was determined to win the prize for the best decorations. It helped that Jay and Stacy were in town for Thanksgiving again while Jim and I headed to Michigan for our annual Cottone/Flora feast. Jay and Stacy decorated Mom's little apartment to rival any NYC Macy's store window. Her artificial tree was festooned with bows and ribbon, sparkling ornaments and twinkle lights. And her door, countertop and table tops, each hosted a cherished decoration from years past. Mom was so proud of their handiwork. All was ready for the Open House.

That afternoon, I picked up some cheese and crackers, Christmas candy, cookies, and punch; all things that Mom liked. Then I picked up Jack from his preschool and headed over to the festivities. With Mom sitting on the couches in the small lounge outside her door, little 4-year-old Jack manned the 3rd Floor lobby elevator, eagerly awaiting anyone who ventured to the floor to check out the decorations for the contest.

Unprompted by me or Mom, he greeted each person with a hearty, "Hi, Come to our party. My Great-grandma has cookies and punch and the best decorations. Follow me, and I will show you." Then, like the best of Maître D's and tour guides, he ushered each person down the hall and through Mom's apartment, pointing out all the decorations, then leading them to the lobby lounge where the cookies and punch were arrayed.

Once they moved down the hall to view other decorations, he'd tally up his total guests. "5…now 8…we had 13 guests, Great Grandma! We're going to win the contest!" Jack got a bigger kick out of that party than anyone else that day. And the guests got an even bigger kick out of him.

Christmas…it really is for children…and the rest of us, too, if we open our hearts enough to recall the light-hearted spirit of childhood.

A Setback

That Christmas at our house, however, brought a setback…

As is our custom, I picked up Mom on the afternoon of Christmas Eve so she could join our family for the celebrations; dinner after an early church service, reflection, carols, and a toddy by the tree before heading to bed and the excitement of gifts and more family in the morning. She was excited about joining us again this year, packing her things in her overnight bag several days in advance.

That evening, her demeanor wasn't out of the ordinary, in fact, she participated in our table banter, joking and flirting with Jim in her usual way. Once the meal concluded, and I was busy with dishes and clean-up, she joined Jim eating several slices of pecan pie with real whipped cream while sitting in her favorite living room chair, before fatigue took over and she retired to our guest room for the night.

Christmas Morning, though, was another story entirely. She awoke disoriented and testy at 11:00 AM. After dressing and joining us in the living room while we waited for Dave and family to arrive, she fretted aloud that she had not bought gifts for anyone. Worse yet, she was angry and upset that she had not heard from our dad. She simply didn't understand why he would ignore her on such an important holiday.

I was able to calm the worry about gifts, telling her I had purchased many she had requested for each of our family, and that we had wrapped them together the evening before.

"Ah," she said. "Yes, I remember now."

But why hadn't Dad called her? Why didn't he get her a gift? Where was he anyway? Over and over and over.

How was I to answer those questions?

I tried the strategy of validating her illusions, a technique I had picked up in the caregiver's support group that Inspired Living hosted on a monthly basis for those of us with loved ones in their facility, but she was having none of it. Christmas was too important to be ignored.

After several rounds of attempting to placate her anguish, Jim gave it another try. "Marcie," he stated gently, somewhat fearful of sending her into fresh grief at the news, "I know where Frank is. He's in heaven. He died in 2004. He's up there watching over all of us right now. He can't be here because he's dead."

She countered in an irritated voice, "Well, I know that, Jim. Of course, he's dead. But why doesn't he call me? Why isn't he here?"

How can you reason with that? Well…you can't. And although Dave's family's arrival and the chaos of gift opening diverted her attention for a time, it did not assuage her anxious worry about Dad. Why was he ignoring her and what happened to the beautiful gifts he usually gave her? Why did he leave her alone on Christmas?

In her increasing illness, Mom's demeanor regarding Dad had softened to a gentleness that was endearing and tender. She'd lost the animosity she previously carried for him and their past, and she yearned for the good times they had together.

My heart broke for her as she puzzled over her feelings of abandonment. It was obvious his death years ago no longer made any sense to her. And my heart broke for me, too, making me miss him more than I had in years.

And Another, and Another, and Another

That January, Mom seemed to enter a new phase, cycling with energy and enthusiasm for life, followed by a bout of what I can only call mania and frantic, unfocused activity, followed by days of delusions and then weeks on end of lethargy and sleepiness. Then, I would notice an upswing in which she emerged into her positive self again, for a time.

She did great when her family was around visiting – hiding her uncertainty and drawing on all her internal resources to interact and show normalcy to visitors. But once they were gone, she would crash. Infrequent visitors may not have noticed, but Jim and I saw her nearly every day, so the swings in energy and lucidity were more obvious to us.

Bed became her preferred retreat. She shunned interaction, but still spent hours on the phone with her cousin, Mary Jane, or her sister, Sally, rehashing the same stories over and over with these patient souls.

We learned in the Dementia Support Group that these cycles were normal, to be expected. A person with the disease of dementia could be impacted positively or negatively by the smallest changes, ones that someone like you or me would not even notice. Things like a small bladder infection, a room that was too hot or too cold, a change in caregivers to someone new on the shift on weekends, heck, even a thunderstorm could throw off a person's equilibrium, and they could go into a downward emotional spiral for days or weeks. That's why consistency was so important for her. That's why moving was a huge disrupter that took her a month or two to absorb.

Nearly a year later (Spring 2017), she faced another change. Mom acquired a suitemate who moved into the second bedroom of her apartment. The arrival of her suitemate, a woman of greater disability than her, was an even more troubling disruption.

We all knew her apartment had an empty second bedroom. We kept the door to that room closed, and that room stood empty for nearly ten months. Because Mom had lived there without a suitemate, she settled into her own routines as though her apartment was solely her own. For months on end, no one was even interested in renting that other room. But no longer.

We could only hope that the arrival would go smoothly.

Due to Mom's new suitemate's declining ability to care for herself, her family arranged for a staff member to take her to the Memory Care unit during the day. They would come to dress her and down the hall they would go, only bringing her back for a change of clothes, if needed, and at night to sleep. Getting used to sharing a common space shouldn't be too much of a disruption, we all thought.

Well, we were mistaken.

It turned out that sleep wasn't part of her new roomie's schedule. Rather, she would cry and scream each night, begging to go home, disrupting everyone within earshot. Mom, ever the nurse, would get up and go in to comfort her, ending up exhausted and frustrated herself before the staff on night duty arrived to quell the commotion.

Mom took to hiding in her own bedroom more and more, curled up on her bed under her big orange, furry throw, not venturing out into the larger living room to avoid a confrontation, even though her suitemate was seldom there. The situation wasn't a compatible one, at all. Yet because Mom's financial resources were growing thinner and thinner, this shared apartment was the best accommodations available to meet both of their needs.

Mom's suitemate's daughter, a psychologist herself, did her best to help her mom get oriented to Inspired Living, and though we seldom saw each other, she made some pretty interesting observations about Mom that she imparted to me in passing.

When I mentioned to her in the lobby one day that I didn't think Mom was delusional most of the time, she offered this observation. "On the contrary. Frequently, when I see your mom in the lobby or in the apartment, she mentions that she's having fun looking at the children over in the corner or that she is waiting for her grandson to pick her up to go strawberry picking with those children over there."

Apparently, happy children were frequent visitors in Mom's imaginary world, though she never spoke about them to me, choosing to keep her little visitors secret. Taking that insight to heart, I did share it with the psychiatric nurse practitioner, who just took note of it, not too alarmed by what she heard. Apparently, this was as my Dad would say "par for the course" in the development of Mom's brain disease.

Warm Blankets and the Spring of Discontent

That spring, Mom retreated even more into herself. She'd lost the ability to work her TV remote or the radio we gave her for Christmas, but she didn't seem to care. She stopped socializing regularly with Connie and the other residents, only interacting during the occasional evening meal, preferring to snooze on her loveseat or snuggle under the covers on her bed for long hours rather than participate in group activities.

Maybe visits from family could pull her out of her doldrums.

Although due to distance and work schedules, Jay and Jill visited a few times per year, Peg and Lynn lived closer and made it a point to visit more often, flying down from their homes in the midwest that spring. And Mom loved their visit!

They took her out to eat, to shop for clothes and for supplies for a craft project they cooked up that was intended to keep her from the boredom that was a constant issue since her most recent retreat into herself. I think Pinterest was the source of this crafty plan, and it was a brilliant one.

Mom would make polar fleece tied blankets for her grandkids. If she could catch on to tying the strips Lynn and Peg cut in the doubled over yards of polar fleece, they hoped it might fill the empty hours.

She made a blanket for Jack that he used his entire Kindergarten year, she made one for Eilee, and another for our cousin Jane's new grandbaby. Then suddenly, her interest waned. "I don't want to tie all those knots anymore, Kathy," she'd say. "It just bores me."

That weeklong visit opened another challenge for we siblings, one that was prompted, I believe, by the new information we received when attending the support group together at Mom's place while Lynn and Peg were in town. The facilitator talked that day about the stages of dementia, and that one had to be careful about overmedicating what may be a natural progression of the disease. Since Lynn has a wealth of medical knowledge and access to medical texts, she took the time when she returned home to review all Mom's medications that her Psychiatric Nurse Practitioner and her new Physicians had prescribed since she entered the facility.

Her conclusion was that maybe Mom was overmedicated and that was causing her deep lethargy and lack of interest in life around her. She asked if I would request a review by the medical team, to see if she could be weaned off any of them. Peg and I both agreed so I made a phone call with the request that we try less medication to see what effect that might have.

My request was met with resistance, but ultimately, she wrote orders to wean Mom off her meds over the course of a week or so. She also engaged in long conversations with Lynn over the phone, conversations that must not have gone too well, because Lynn conveyed to me that her concerns were met with scorn.

Somehow, I ended up in the middle of that one, with Mom's Nurse Practitioner calling me one morning to complain on and on about the decision and what it might do for Mom's wellbeing. From my layperson's perspective, I was concerned, too, but trusted our perception that medication could be zoning her out.

We were all waiting to see the outcome of our decision.

We'll see in a bit, I thought. We'll know if she's more with-it without the psych meds.

Oh, she was with-it, alright, and very quickly became a terror on wheels.

Where Are My Hearing Aids?

Seems like a simple question, right?

But no, this was a demand…first shouted at Adrianne, Mom's morning caregiver, then screamed at her down the hall as she strode to the locked medication cart to retrieve the precious cargo, stored there overnight since Mom so often lost them somewhere in her bedcovers or couch cushions.

"Where are my hearing aids?!"

Then, Mom loudly punctuated her demand with a display of pique she had never shown before.

While hollering at the top of her lungs, she stood in the hallway, tearing off all her clothes. Finally, standing naked outside her apartment door, she demanded her hearing aids this instant.

Well…we wanted to see what removing the psych meds would do, right?

Yep! If they were helping manage outbursts like this, or worse, it was probably time to reinstate her previous medication regime.

Mom's Path

By now, Mom seemed to be struggling mightily to retain her former self.

She wanted to please us by making those baby blankets, but really, she preferred to lay on her bed in the reverie of her mind, walking through memories that cropped up in jumbled form, sending her on a day or a week of delusion. At least the memories were no longer frightening. She went back to happier times in her mind, sometimes creating events out of a thread here and a thread there, until she designed an internal life that only she could see but that seemed entirely real and fulfilling to her.

Visits from Jack were a touchpoint to remind her of the real world. He seemed to read her spirit, sensing she could respond to his embrace. So, when I brought him to see her, he would immediately kick off his shoes and hop up on her bed, crawling under the fluffy orange blanket to snuggle her, offering her his Georgie, the stuffed monkey, to hold. She would sigh in contentment and hum to him, a wordless song I remember my own grandmother using to soothe her grandbabies in her kitchen rocking chair.

Mom seemed content to live primarily in her mind. That is, until the med switch. Then, her buried emotions came roaring to the fore. She had no capacity or resources to stop them. Her brain disease had robbed her of the control the meds were intended to help restore. She needed those supplemental chemicals to try to preserve what she had left.

My Path

What I later learned was that new behaviors could come on at any time with this disease. The reduction or switch of meds could have caused her outburst...or not. New plateaus of ability followed by downturns in behavior can come and go. So, too, can rocky times with care staff and the medical team. The key to all of it is communication.

It was important to keep open channels of communication with the medical team, sharing concerns openly and discussing alternatives to the established care routines. This was a complex illness, fraught with twists and turns that were unexpected and alarming at times. Having trust in the professionals chosen for Mom's care was essential to everyone's peace of mind.

But it seemed as if this trust was starting to fray. We knew Mom best, after all. *Right?*

It was also critical, I discovered, to spend more quality time with Mom, in order to follow the ups and downs of her moods, her abilities, and her state of mind. I stopped in daily at random times to check in on her and to interact with her and the staff. It was important to watch for what enlivened her and what irritated her, to notice changes in her treatment, and to help support the care staff by keeping with their established routines and protocols as much as possible.

And, I found, it was important for her to have soothing physical contact, a soft touch, a snuggly Georgie and Jack, a kiss on the forehead all calmed her, letting her know she was loved.

I needed that time with her so that I could be a strong advocate for her with her team of ever-revolving care members and her medical team. And to find that time, I dropped many of my own outside commitments in order pay closer attention to her changing needs.

This is important work, I thought. More important than most of the other things I had in mind for myself.

As unsettling as her care could be, I felt it was a gift to spend this nurturing time with her. I was the one who was being blessed. I felt a distinct and deliberate Call, one I heard clearly and was moved to fulfill – so my friends, my workout routines and volunteer roles were redirected to the back burner for a season. Most understood, and if they didn't, well, I would never know, would I?

But I will always be able to cherish this uniquely Spirit-blessed time with Mom.

Chapter Fifteen:
Night Nurse and The Bus to Memory Care

When I arrived one afternoon to visit Mom, the Director spotted me entering the building and asked to speak with me.

"Kathy," he said as we sat in their conference room, "we found your mother wandering in the parking lot, trying to get to a bus stop to return home to Michigan. She said it was because it was the end of her nursing shift. This is not the first time we noticed her wandering, although it is the first time she got this far into the parking lot. I want you to know that we have observed your mom becoming more delusional in the past little while. We decided to move her over to a respite room in the Memory Care wing until you decide if that would be the best choice to keep her safe while she lives with us here at Inspired Living."

"Wow! Thank you so much for catching her before she got too far! She could have wandered away never to be seen again or tried to cross Highway 70 and gotten killed!" I was stunned!

Unable to sleep, she had been watching the 7:00 AM staff shift change from a seat in the lobby for weeks, the Director told me. She must have figured out how to step outside and make a run for it without notice in the normal flow of people coming and going at the beginning of the day.

She didn't intend to cause undue alarm, she just wanted to catch the bus, to get home from her own nursing shift at Providence Hospital where she had spent the night caring for her charges. She was tired and wanted to wait for that bus that would take her down Outer Drive in Dearborn then down Jefferson Avenue to her home in River Rouge, MI.

Had she been able to fulfill her plans, she could have easily gotten lost, or she could have ended up on a very busy, state highway which was only a block and a half away.

And…this wasn't the first time she had tried to walk out of the facility or the first time the Director encountered this delusion. Just a few days before, he recounted, she had come into his office demanding to give the report at the end of her nursing shift then be paid for her time worked. She told him in no uncertain terms that she had completed her commitment to this hospital, now they had to complete theirs. She was so insistent, he ended up writing her a fake check for her time on the ward where she supposedly worked as an RN. Once she was satisfied that she received what was due her, he called a caregiver on the floor to escort her to dinner.

When I was with her, she was often silent or repeated the same conversations she knew were safe or familiar, or alternately, I found her sleeping regardless of time of day. She did sound like she was living in a delusion from time-to-time. But we could still communicate as though everything was normal. I did not suspect that things were dramatically different when I wasn't there.

Apparently, though, she was now acting on her delusions. The Director and I agreed that I would consult with my family and with the Psychiatric Nurse Practitioner, then make a decision on what to do going forward. Gratefully, he told me that she could stay in the respite room in Memory Care for as long as a week or two and that they did have a permanent room for her in that wing should we so choose.

I knew what I thought, but everyone else deserved a chance to weigh in. Memory Care was a big change, a bit costlier than her assisted living arrangement, and more importantly, another reluctant step into the fog of dementia, even if it was what the professionals advised.

All Hands on Deck

Back and forth, back and forth went the phone calls across geography, weighing varying perceptions of need and the intense desire to keep Mom's care consistent. Finally, I secured everyone's agreement that Memory Care was the next step, though I am not sure it settled well with each of my siblings.

Okay, I thought, let's move. It's the only option to ensure Mom's safety, even if we don't want to admit that her illness has moved into another stage, one we hoped we could somehow avoid.

As timing would have it, our son, Mark, was in Florida for a few weeks going through management training for a new position, and Dave had Saturday off the coming week. The guys could help Jim and me with the move, handling it easily with the dolly and cart the facility provided. I called the Director and booked the move for Saturday. It wouldn't take long, as she was only moving into another wing. Her new room was close, really just down the hall and through a set of locked doors, but it was lightyears from the freedom she had experienced before.

It was all hands on deck. Jim and I found her new bedroom furniture that fit better in her new space, and our guys rallied in the parking lot, setting up a plan. We were done in three hours.

What struck me as we settled her into her new room, a spacious double room with a large closet and bath, was she didn't notice her new space was behind locked doors. We never called her new location "Memory Care", and she never figured that out.

She accepted her new room without complaint. She seemed content to accept the extra supervision and assistance offered by the care staff, even forging a warm relationship with one of the team members, Matt.

Mom would say, "He's so darling. I wish he was young enough for Peggy. And, Kathy, he's a twin, and he is studying for his RN. That's why we get along so well. He understands me."

It didn't matter to her that he was in his 20's and Peg was in her

60's. To Mom, always thinking of her kids as kids, this would be a perfect match. She would do anything for Matt – dress for breakfast, take her shower, go play Bingo, wear her hearing aids. Matt was the man!

Suspicion – Someone is Stealing My Chico's Outfits

One April morning, I buzzed into the unit and walked down the hall into Mom's room to find everything in disarray. She had taken her lamps apart, stashed lampshades and lightbulbs in her Chinese chest, an antique she used as her coffee table. She took all her clothes out of the closet, stuffed them in bags and strewed them across the floor. All her pictures were hidden inside socks or under PJ's in her drawers, and her suitcases were open on the bed which was stripped of all its bedding.

"What's up, Mom?"

"Oh, I'm packing, Kathy. I was up all night. I need to be ready to go on our trip. I am getting ready to go. When is the taxi picking us up? I have my ticket right here somewhere."

"Not until after lunch, Mom," I countered, flabbergasted at the mess and heartsick at this latest delusion. *How could I help her through this one?* "Let Matt take you down to have lunch, and I'll be there in while to join you."

While Matt rescued her from her self-created chaos, I stayed behind to put everything back in order. It took me a full hour to right the room again. But I had to laugh. When she was determined, she could work wonders overnight.

I had recently been reminded in the caregiver's support group that if Mom was living out a delusion, I should play along, but to try to divert her attention with another activity. Especially helpful was learning of an unusual brain response to walking through a doorway to another room. Apparently, passing through that natural demarcation from room to room shifts the thinking of the patient, allowing a break in the looping delusional thought. That's why lunch was so essential, not so much for the food, but for the transition from one room to another, from her room to the hallway and through the archway to the cafeteria, all used as an attempt to break her insistence that a trip was in the offing.

I read how those nearing the end of life start talking about taking trips, start putting things in order to be ready for their journey. I wondered to myself if her packing had any linkage to that phenomena.

Who knew about the inner workings of the mind? It was both baffling and fascinating to watch. But it was also sad to stand witness to the unraveling of a vital human spirit.

Each new revelation, each new behavior, each twist and turn in this disease was gut-wrenching. I had to stay in the moment, stay present in the now, rather than try to figure out a reason or purpose for this suffering. Otherwise, I would lose my ability to help.

Another day, I was greeted by Mom in a tizzy.

"Kathy, someone has been stealing my clothes. I cannot find my Chico's outfits. I had three of them, you know the ones. Now they are gone. Those damn girls who come in here are taking my stuff. They are just the right size, you know. If I find them, I am going to kick their ass!"

Oh my! Something else new. This particular expletive was not in her usual vernacular, but the support group facilitator had informed us that once other language skills fade, those from our early years survive. She'd told us, "As the part of the brain that governs socially-acceptable behavior shrinks, the filters are off. Anything may come out, so don't be surprised."

I spent the better part of the afternoon searching for her precious, Chico's Traveler's sets, black pants, shells and jackets that she counted as her best outfits. I went with a care staff member to the laundry and sorted through the baskets of dirty and clean clothes. No dice. I returned to Mom's room and carefully went through all her drawers, looked in her suitcase and any remaining bags I had not taken home after the last incident. Still no dice. I sorted hanger-by-hanger through her closet. *Hmmm, why was that raincoat so heavy? Well...wouldn't you know it.* Mom had hung her Chico's outfits, every last one of them, under that raincoat, then buttoned it up so they were not visible to the casual observer. Unfortunately, they weren't visible to her, either.

In her mind, someone stole them. After all, she couldn't find them, so they must be gone.

Sparkling Like Pink Champagne

I don't want to convey that all was grim and frightening or anger-producing for Mom. Day-to-day reality was primarily routine, punctuated by incidents that could be frustrating, but often were endearing.

One I remember fondly was a day I arrived to pick her up for the hair and nail appointments I had set for her at outside salons. It was one of our favorite monthly excursions together, usually wrapped up by a lunch at a fast food restaurant to get her fries and a hamburger, something she frequently craved.

That morning, she wasn't dressed when I arrived and had not yet eaten breakfast. I helped her get dressed and sent her to breakfast with one of the care staff, while I straightened up her room and picked up all her candy wrappers and tissues.

When she returned twenty minutes later, she would not leave unless I found her birthday crown. "I want to look pretty for my party," she said. "I want to sparkle like pink champagne!"

We found that precious plastic crown from her 90th Birthday Party in the back of one of her drawers, and she plopped it on top of her head. "Okay, I'm ready to go, Kathy."

She wore that crown into the beauty shop and into the nail salon next door, where she reveled in the gentle care the nail technicians always offered, treating someone of her elder status with deep respect. They smiled, asking if it was her birthday. "Yes," she said. "I am sparkling today for my birthday."

Later, she asked me to take her shopping for a skirt and top to wear to her imaginary party.

Sure, why not?

We found a gauzy white skirt and a luscious peach top – perfect in her mind for the upcoming events.

The checkout person noticed the crown and congratulated her on her birthday, her 92nd, though it was really months away. Then, she bent down rummaging under the counter for something, popping up with a plastic scepter in her hand, streamers flowing from the colorful disk at the top. "Happy Birthday, Darling," she gushed. "This will go perfectly with your crown."

Mom accepted the gift with delight! She waved that scepter all the way home.

I would not be surprised if she has it stashed away in a special place to this day. It wasn't her birthday or even her birthday month, but what difference did it make? Celebrating it made her happy.

It made her sparkle like pink champagne.

The Boyfriend, The Beatles and Hawaii Bound

Mom's mind was busy working overtime.

She said she had trouble sleeping at night, but she slept often and long during the day. When she was lucid, I could never imagine she needed a Memory Care Unit. She would converse clearly, ask about specific family members and chat knowledgably about current events. But the delusions were becoming more frequent, and even more fantastical, although completely out of touch with today.

Early one morning, she called, admonishing me to hurry up and get dressed because her new boyfriend was going to pick up me and Jim in his helicopter in ten minutes. He was going to take us to their wedding in Hawaii.

When I inquired further about this new boyfriend, I heard quite a story...

"He's been hiding here, Kathy. The staff has kept him hidden because he has too much money, and they don't want anyone to steal it. But I found out about him, and now we are getting married. He owns a business in northern Michigan, an entire real estate development, and his helicopter will be there to get you right away. Don't forget to dress up, Kathy."

Surprisingly, some of those threads of thought had links to her past. Mom always said she wanted to find a rich husband. Well, now she'd snagged one. She used to live in The Villages near Ocala, FL, a development started by a real estate mogul from northern Michigan. And, she loved Hawaii. She and Dad had traveled there often with a bankers' group back when Dad was riding high in his career. Funny how she'd scrambled all those elements into this exciting adventure.

"Okay, Mom, I'll be ready when he gets here. By the way, I plan to stop by around 1:00 today, Okay? I'll be there after lunch."

To her, the conflicting plans made sense. When I got to her place at 1:00, she never mentioned the boyfriend, though my sisters each said she had called them, too. We were ALL going to the wedding... sometime.

Another morning, another bubbly, excited phone call. "Hey, Kathy, you're late. We have to hurry because we're going to miss The Beatle's concert. I have the tickets right here in my purse, but we'll miss it if you don't get here in a few minutes. Hurry Up!"

"Sure, Mom. I love The Beatles! I'll be right over."

When I was a little 11-year-old girl, I loved The Beatles. I knew the words to all their songs, still do. I dreamed teeny-bopper dreams of marrying Paul McCartney. We were living in a Philadelphia suburb at the time, and Mom and Dad even arranged home plate tickets for my sister and me to attend the first Beatle's concert in the US at Shea Stadium in New York City. They left us at the gate to join the other screaming fans for the evening while they took my other siblings to the 1964 Worlds' Fair.

Now, Mom was back there, time-traveling, offering me another opportunity of a lifetime.

Not My Reading Machine!

Indicators of her declining capacity came rapidly now.

The reading machine she'd used for years to supplement her failing eyesight seemed to her a foreign object.

"Someone stole my reading machine, Kathy," she'd complain. "This is not my reading machine."

When we moved her to the Memory Care Unit, we decided to place her machine on her desk, rather than move its rickety printer stand. The desk was sturdier, I reasoned. Not a good idea. Mom's mind recognized the old configuration, a machine resting on top of a rickety printer stand. Since it no longer rested there, it must not be hers.

Compounding her confusion was the realization she could not figure out how to use this foreign contraption that took up so much space on her desk.

"I know how to use mine," she'd say. "This one is different. I guess I will have to get used to it, but it's not mine. Someone stole the one I had. You better go look in my other room, Kathy. I bet you forgot to move it, and someone stole it."

Not only had she lost the capacity to use an essential tool for her day-to-day functioning, she couldn't even recognize it because it didn't look the same to her when sitting on a different piece of furniture.

Yes, something had been stolen, but by her disease, not by some unknown thief.

The executive functioning that we all took for granted was fading, stealing from Mom her capacity to reason, to recognize objects and to follow simple steps to complete familiar tasks.

This disease was a thief, alright.

Yes, Mom, you're right.

Mom's Path

Mom's internal life was primarily rich and joyful.

When I opted to follow her lead, buying into her playful, imaginary experiences, it was a wild but often delightful ride. The problem was the joy was often tempered by new and very real frustrations. And I had to go along with those, too, waiting until the fog cleared and she forgot her obsession with the topic of the hour – new makeup to complement her face lift, even though that surgery was 45 years ago; a new reading machine, since the one sitting on her desk can't possibly be hers; those darn girls, stealing her clothes, even though the clothes always showed up in her closet or under other items in her underwear drawer.

Each day brought a new frustration. Yet, when she had to, she could rally her internal resources to act appropriately in any situation.

In the coming summer, we would observe that capacity over and over and over again.

My Path

I have to admit I enjoyed some of Mom's delusions.

I found them to be fascinating windows into the workings of her internal life, often showing a humorous side of her I never saw growing up. Granted, they weren't based in reality, but they were often funny, joyful or quirky enough to make me laugh out loud.

We had fun together, even when she was a bit out of touch. There was no harm in supporting her current reality until she returned to the mundane existence in Memory Care. It made life easier for both of us.

Her frustrations were another story. All I could do was promise to help in any way I could while waiting until that particular obsession ceased to torment her.

More and more, I felt like I was parenting my own parent; caring for a toddler-like, fragile soul, one who pinned all her hope and trust in what I thought, what I could do to provide for her, when I came to see her and what I could do to chase away the ghosts under her bed.

It was a broad responsibility, an important role… one I knew I was intended to hold, one I could not do without the help of my husband and family, a deliberate Call to respond, to learn and to grow.

Part V: A Season of Goodbye

Chapter Sixteen:
Summer Storms

May Day

W hile sitting at church one Saturday night, Jim and I got a call from Lynn.

Aunt Sally, Mom's dear younger sister who came to Florida as a snowbird with our Uncle Mike every winter, had a stroke and was being transported to a Tampa hospital. While they were dressing for Saturday night Mass, she suffered a catastrophic bleed in her brain. She was only 83, and as vital as anyone would ever want to be.

This wasn't fair. This wasn't right. This wasn't something I could tell Mom until we knew more about the outcome.

Sally went home to God on the evening of May 1st, resting in His arms from the very Hospice House where she had completed training as a volunteer only two weeks before. Our God took care of her and Mike in her last hours, bringing her home on the day dedicated to Christ's mother Mary, to whom Sally had a lifelong devotion.

When I told Mom the next day, she showed little emotion, but she shared an observation of gratitude that comforted her. "At least she went on May Day," she said. "She was always dedicated to Our Blessed Mother."

"Yes, Mom, she's at peace now. She's at peace."

Weeks later, Jim and I flew with Mom to Michigan to join our entire family and all their friends for the Celebration of Life. That day, Mom was on. She was aware, participating appropriately in the service and the luncheon. She spoke with family and remembered and reminisced with friends from long, long ago, recounting funny stories and pouring over pictures posted throughout the gathering hall.

I was grateful we decided to make the trip with her, against the advice that travel could cause a setback in her condition. It was a precious family time, a mixture of deep grief and an even deeper love.

Who was I to deny her this good bye...

Find Me a Resting Place - Bring Dad Home

Her sister Sally's death, however, triggered another obsession.

Mom worried day-after-day about her own resting place. She wanted to make sure her funeral was pre-planned. Wanted to ensure she would have a choice now, so she would be ready when it was her turn to go.

We talked and talked about it, on trips to Walmart, to the nail salon, sitting out on the lanai on her floor. It worried her. She wanted to make sure I knew her wishes. She wanted to be cremated, and she wanted to be with Dad.

I had learned earlier that year about the Sarasota National Cemetery, a spectacularly beautiful place of honor for deceased veterans and those who lost their lives in combat. Through research, I learned that Dad was eligible to be interred there, either in a columbarium or in a gravesite, within the rows and rows of stately white headstones, declaring for the generations his devotion to our country in a time of war.

When I talked with Mom about it, she encouraged me to move forward to have Dad's ashes moved to the newly-opened cemetery. When she died, she, too, would have a place of honor with her own inscription on the opposite side of his headstone. This pleased her.

I made arrangements for Dad's move and interment, with full military honors, scheduling the ceremony for mid-August.

On the day of Dad's ceremony, it rained all morning. But by 3:00, the clouds cleared, blown away by winds that quickened across the open cemetery fields. Our small band – Mom, Jim, Dave and me – were met at the information center by a guide, one who explained to us what would happen at the Interment Shelter, that we could offer prayers and words of honor if we chose, and that he would be with us every step of the way from the arrival of the honor guard until Dad's ashes were once again at rest where he truly belonged, in among his fellow Marines.

Mom sat at attention, flanked by Jim and David, as the flag was unfurled and taps echoed through the air. She watched, eyes rapt, as the young Marines of the honor guard carefully folded the flag and presented it to her. Surprising us all at how present she was, she rose then, stepping lightly to the urn resting on a granite pedestal, flag embraced in her arms. Movingly, she slowly bent down and gently kissed the top of the vessel holding her husband of 52 years.

A Hurricane of the Heart

On a brilliant Florida fall day, I sat in the sunshine of an outdoor café. My two new friends and I chatted amiably about trivial things, until one asked me, "How're you doing now that your Mom has moved away?"

I know she expected to hear a string of positive comments, maybe that I was rested, grateful for the reprieve, happy that someone else was now taking the burden of her care. Instead, I sighed and said, "Not too well. I'm sad. I feel kinda empty, lost. We didn't really have a chance to say goodbye."

That was it. Mom was gone…to Indiana…living with my older sister while she looked for a suitable new residence for her.

From my raw perspective, the change was too fast, completely unexpected and felt altogether out of my control. You know by now that I have never been one who liked relinquishing control, even of those things that really were out of my control in the first place.

So…let me back up here…and share the entire story…

Harvey, Irma, Security Shattered

The news and weather reports grew ever more ominous throughout the last weeks of August 2017.

A swirling tropical system swelled into the largest rainmaker in hurricane history. What became Hurricane Harvey decimated the Texas coast and the city of Houston and flooded the surrounding suburbs. We watched in horror, along with the rest of the world, as the flood waters inundated home after home after home. The trauma unfolding was palpable. Memories of Hurricane Katrina came rushing back. This could not be happening again in one of the largest cities in Texas. But it was, and the unease seized our collective imagination like turnpike drivers rubbernecking a horrific car crash.

What if it had happened to us?

That was the backdrop as I opened the mail one afternoon to a mini-hurricane of our own.

I received a letter from Mom's Psychiatric Nurse Practitioner informing her patients' care partners that she would no longer treat residents at the facility where Mom lived. Her reasons were stated obscurely but they held the implication that it would be a good idea to seek another home for Mom, citing serious disagreements with the management about her access to residents.

Did Mom's medical provider really believe the new privacy policies restricting access to patient files were concerning to the point of her being unable to guarantee quality care? That's what I wondered, trying to read between the lines of the strange letter. If they could not offer that assurance, what did that mean for Mom?

I met with the Interim Director and the Manager of the Memory Care Unit to express my concern and listen to their side of the situation. They had legitimate reasons for the new policy, rightly insisting that staff follow corporate policy and privacy regulations.

Still, after consultation with my four siblings, I began a determined research project. I visited the alternative Memory Care facilities suggested by Mom's Nurse Practitioner and those within a few miles of our home, in case we did find it important to find a new place for Mom. I narrowed down the search to two good possibilities, with similar care standards and available accommodations we could afford.

I arranged lunchtime visits with Mom at each facility so she could get a feel for the staff, the environment and most importantly, the residents, just in case she wanted to explore a new place to live, one she picked herself. If we did decide we had to move her, we didn't want her to feel she was being forced again into one we chose for her under duress.

At each, she expressed initial enthusiasm, stating how lovely and homey they were. Predictably, though, after several of these visits, she grew tired of the exploration. Her mind melded the facilities into one incoherent picture, and none of them now looked or felt comfortable. Some seemed fantastic, some very pleasant, with familiar faces from her former facility, but none perfect. The thought of moving was just too overwhelming.

The weather made the decision for us.

Mother Nature had other plans.

The Brewing Storm

While we stewed about the right thing to do, the eyes of the country shifted from Houston and Hurricane Harvey's devastation to a new threat on the verge of blowing up to a full-scale crisis.

Looming out in the Atlantic basin churned Irma, one of the largest, strongest hurricanes ever recorded, inching ever closer to the Florida peninsula. By Labor Day weekend, it was obvious that this monster storm was going to wreak havoc throughout our state.

The spaghetti models shifted hour-by-hour, sending chills throughout our community when they converged on the Gulf Coast, predicting a Category 5 bull's eye hit right over our home town.

What was unique with this storm, however, was its enormity. From eye to feeder bands, its potential destructive path encompassed the entire Florida peninsula. No matter where it made landfall, people would suffer, and homes, property, and potentially lives would be lost.

Eleven years had passed since a major hurricane made landfall on the Florida Gulf Coast. Our experience back then was one of minor inconvenience, not destruction. Now, Jim and I had a decision to make. Should we ride out the storm in our second-floor condo on the marsh, with open water to the river, then the Gulf itself? Should we trust that Mom would be alright at Inspired Living, knowing they had experienced some flooding a few weeks before, when we had an unusual 11-inch rainstorm?

Her facility had activated strong disaster plans ensuring adequate caregiver support throughout the storm, so it was possible for her to shelter in place with the "C team" and their families, if we so chose.

Our own decision was soon made for us. We lived in Zone A. For those outside of hurricane-prone areas, Zone A is a mandatory evacuation zone, more prone to flooding or storm surge devastation than other areas on the map due to the proximity to bodies of water.

Our choices were few. Stay and defy the recommendations of public safety officials, go to a shelter set up in our town or get the heck out of dodge before the monster hit. After learning that our son planned to evacuate with Jackson, Jack's mom, Lindsey, her mother and her toddler daughter Jo Jo, we made a decision. We would rent a vacation house outside the predicted danger zone near Atlanta, Georgia so that we could all shelter together. It was just too stressful to think of loved ones enduring this storm without being there with them.

Evacuation by car would not be good for Mom or her fragile mental state. The chaos of the long car ride and staying with such a motley crew of our disjointed family members seemed to me to be too much for her to bear given her fear of thunderstorms and her need for consistent routine. Yet, I was not willing to leave her alone in our city without us, in case the predicted hurricane path proved accurate.

Would it be possible to send her to Lynn's house in Indiana for a few days until things settled back to normal?

On Monday, September 4th, I called to my sister to ask.

It was a short conversation.

She agreed to take Mom into her home until the danger passed but could not pick her up at the airport until Thursday the 7th. Time was getting short. Landfall was predicted for Saturday night the 10th or early Sunday morning. Flights were quickly filling up, but that was the best either of us could do on such short notice. We booked Mom on one of the last Southwest flights available out of Tampa early Thursday morning, anticipating her return the following Tuesday.

Then Jim and I made preparations to secure our own home before we picked her up. At the last minute, we booked a hotel near the airport for Wednesday night because it was too uncertain to wait until Thursday morning.

I didn't know if she would remember that we were leaving, and why. I did not want to wrestle with her moods and reluctance to leave the warm covers of her bed in the morning to get her dressed for a flight and out the door on time, risking missing her flight to safety.

The hotel gave us one of their last remaining rooms, the hallway door looking out over a waist-high railing to the inside courtyard eight floors down. It was a precarious spot for a woman prone to night wandering. As protection from any inadvertent catastrophe, Jim slept on the lumpy, old pull-out couch guarding the door while

I shared a bed with Mom in the adjoining room.

Every hour or so, she would pop up, startled awake when I moved or changed positions. I reassured her that I was right there, and she was safe. We got very little sleep. It was a long night for all three of us.

The next morning, Tampa International Airport buzzed with a mix of anxiety and relief as families said hurried goodbyes to loved ones escaping the storm by air. After surreptitiously alerting the gate crew that Mom – legally blind, hard of hearing and with dementia – was traveling alone and may need extra assistance, I stood chatting with her in the boarding line, trying not to show my own impatience to get on the road while there was still gas available for our drive, at the same time, hoping to distract her enough to keep her calm.

Two cups of hot chocolate, a trip to the ladies' room and two candy bars later, we finally heard the announcement, "Pre-boarding for the flight to Indianapolis for those needing assistance." From the line of fifteen or more wheelchairs queuing behind Mom, it looked like almost everyone would need to pre-board.

It was quite a testament to the gate and flight crew, who seemingly unfazed by the tension around them, exhibited good humor and compassion as they welcomed these elderly and infirm passengers onboard. *Thanks, Southwest!*

I gave Mom her ticket to hold, confirmed that Lynn would be waiting at the gate for her at the other end of the flight and kissed her quickly on the forehead. Then, I watched as the attendant wheeled her onto the plane, feeling relief that she would be safe from the storm and from the physical and emotional turmoil that a car evacuation might cause her.

And I can't lie. It was a huge relief for Jim and me, too. Car travel with Mom could be a struggle. Now that she would be safe with Lynn, we could juggle the demands of evacuation without worrying about Mom's needs.

Good thing, too. That road trip was unbelievable!

Jim and I left Tampa, hitting the road around noon, not a car to be seen ahead of us on Interstate 75. *Had everyone else already gone? Were we too late to find gas and make it out of danger?* Anxiety turned my stomach into knots. We fretted as our gas gauge crept toward *E*. Going on intuition, Jim left the highway and discovered some rationed gas in a little town outside of Gainesville, Florida. At a rundown, rural station, the owner and two other volunteers policed the growing line with military precision.

"Ten dollars only, then off you go!"

"Three gallons each, no more. That is all I have left. Three gallons – cash only."

"Thanks, man!"

How far would that take us?

The trip to northern Georgia is usually a piece of cake. It should have taken nine to ten hours. It took sixteen – all our patience, extreme bladder control, and the remains of our cell phone data depleted by our often-inaccessible GPS, we were exhausted before we pulled into our rented refuge. It was a grueling drive, teaching us to take nothing for granted – technology, our vehicles, ready food, water and sanitary bathrooms – all in question along the way.

Fellow travelers did provide a bright spot. We were all in this together – thumbs up along the highway. Irma, be damned!

Five days of wavering between uncertainty and hope followed. In the last few hours leading up to landfall, Irma took a turn twenty miles inland, destroying lives and livelihoods in the Florida Keys and inland counties, sparing Sarasota/Bradenton from the worst. Still, many took enormous losses to their homes and businesses. Debris filled the streets, power lines lay twisted in the wreckage.

Despite warnings on social media that gas was unavailable and traffic atrocious, I, for one, could not stand waiting and wondering what would greet us when we got back. All I wanted was to get out of Georgia and get back home...Now!

We were some of the lucky ones. We arrived home to very little damage, just a freezer full of spoiled food and one tree toppled by the wind. We had power. Our family was safe, and our home intact.

Breathing a deep sigh that had been building for days, we started plans to bring Mom home from Indiana. It was time to settle back to normal life.

Yes, we were okay. We were home.

Homecoming?

We planned Mom's return for the following Thursday. That gave her memory care facility time to reestablish routines after hosting residents, staff and family members for a week during the storm. I received a text from Lynn earlier the prior week:

Got Mom's flight (not me). They were going fast and up in price. She will leave Thurs. Sept 21 at 9:30 and get into Tampa at 11:45 AM. It is flight 1428 for $180.

Perfect. Thanks! I replied.

I think we all were ready to return to normal, Lynn included. Mom would fly home unaccompanied in a couple of days. I marked the date in my calendar, reserving plenty of time to greet her at the airport gate and get her settled again.

A frantic phone call Sunday morning put everything we planned into question...

It was early, about 6:30 AM so you can imagine the charge of fear that ran through me as I lunged for the phone. *Was someone hurt? Was there an accident?* Oh, Shit! I thought, reverting to one of Mom's crude expletives. *What if it's Mom?*

It was Peg on the line. My younger sister had driven down from her home in Michigan for the weekend to visit with Mom, Lynn and her husband Lowen while Mom was in town.

I will never forget the electric emotion in her voice on that call.

"Kathy," she said, "Oh my God! Mom is a lot worse than we thought! She seemed perfectly fine the whole time I was here. But whoa! She really needs to be in Memory Care. You will never believe what she did. We had no idea she was this bad!" Words tumbled over words as she tried to express the distress she was feeling.

Lynn chimed in, "She almost gave us a heart attack!"

"What?! What?! Is she Okay?" was all I could manage. "Tell me what's going on."

As it turns out, Mom went off to bed Saturday night a little later than her usual early time, around 10:00 PM. She and my sisters had stayed up talking after a full day trying out the baking recipes Mom remembered from her childhood and our family years. It had been a fun, satisfying visit. She was animated and talkative, telling stories of her days in her own mother and father's home and of her grandfather's house and business.

So, when she finally fell asleep, Peg, Lynn, and Lowen thought she would be out soundly until noon the next day, no sweat. But that was not to be.

Sometime between 3:45 and 4:00 AM, Mom woke up, certain she heard a fire alarm going off. Without waking anyone or asking for help, she got herself dressed, put in her own hearing aids, brushed her hair and teeth in the guest hall bathroom, and using her walker to steady herself, she made her way down the hallway from the guest room to the front door.

She maneuvered the deadbolt on the heavy, wooden front door, opened it and pushed open the storm door. Walker in hand, she made her own way across the front porch, down two brick steps and across the walkway pavers to the driveway.

But she didn't stop there...

She walked down the sloped driveway, around the circle in the street to the house next door, up their drive, across their front walkway, up two more steps, across their porch and rang their doorbell several times.

A nearly-blind woman. IN THE DARK! At 4:00 in the morning!

It took several tries to rouse the neighbors, but when they did come to the door, it must have been startling to see a tiny woman with a walker standing there.

She said to them, "Will you help me? There is an alarm going off next door, and I need someone because no one has turned it off."

Can you even imagine what the man who answered the door was thinking?

These were neighbors Lynn and Lowen didn't know well. Their paths rarely crossed since both couples were still working. But they got Mom to come inside. They suspected she may be from next door, as the wife had seen Lynn with Mom in the car a few times, but just to be sure, they did what any concerned Good Samaritan would do….they called the police.

They chatted with Mom until the officer came. Apparently, she was a delightful conversationalist while waiting for the cops.

Back at my sister's house, everyone was still asleep. Peg was upstairs in the loft bedroom, while Lynn and Lowen were asleep in the master suite on the other side of the house. Then, their phone rang.

As Lynn tells it, a mother's instinct kicked in immediately. *Was someone hurt? Was it one of the kids in an accident?* Sound familiar? And the voice on the other end of the line did nothing to assuage her fear. "Is this Ms. Stewart? This is Officer Peterson from the Noblesville Police Department …. Is your Mom?"… then a pause, "Oh, just come to the front door."

Heart pounding in her throat, Lynn threw on a robe and rushed to open the front door. There stood the officer, next to our little 4'11" Mom with her walker.

"Mom! What are you doing out there?!" Lynn exclaimed.

If it hadn't been so dangerous, it would be hilarious. But this was deathly serious. Mom's dementia had shown itself after twelve days of her mentally and emotionally working overtime to hide her symptoms. At least that's how I saw it. She really did hear an alarm, though there was no alarm system in the house. She handled it in a reasoned way, though her actions weren't appropriate to the situation. She did ask for help, just not in the way that you or I would.

What I heard from Lynn and Peg was almost beyond belief, yet I had seen it all before, or most of it. I was so relieved that she wasn't hurt and glad that both Peg and Lynn were together to support each other when it happened. Lowen was the coolest head. He went right out to Home Depot as soon as it opened to purchase a house alarm that shrieked loudly when anyone crossed the invisible electronic barrier it threw across the hallway threshold.

Time for True Confessions

While they were recounting their harrowing morning, my own emotions roiled. I had so many reactions...yes, relief, but also amusement at Mom's ingenuity and spunk. I had empathy for Peg, Lynn and Lowen's distress, and of course, love for my fierce Mom, who somehow always figured out a way through whatever she was facing – as quirky and jaw-dropping as her solutions often were.

Perhaps it was bad of me to think this, but in a way, I was glad it happened. Although they clearly denied it, I still harbored a niggling suspicion way back in my mind that my sisters thought I exaggerated when describing Mom's symptoms. A part of me thought that maybe now they would completely understand what I had been trying to explain to them from afar for the past few years. Now they were living it, too. You can't deny that knock on the door in the middle of the night.

"She needs to be in Memory Care," they said.

There, we are all on the same page. All doubts, if there were any, had been erased.

Then came the bombshell, at least it seemed so to me at the time...

Still on the call, though in a much calmer tone now, Peg spoke up, "Kathy, we think you have had Mom for long enough. We know now how hard you and Jim had to work at her care, and we think we should take it on now."

Lynn broke in, "Kath, I think Lowen and I should have Mom up here permanently. She has been here now for long enough that Florida is just a memory to her. She is comfortable here. We have much more family around to help, and Peg is just three hours away. We can handle it together and take the burden off you. It has been a lot for you and Jim, and it has not been good for your health. I am canceling Mom's flight, and I'll look for a Memory Care facility nearby so that we can take over her care."

Just like that. Decision made. No "What do you think? No, "Let's try this temporarily." Just like that, "We're keeping Mom here."

I should have been thrilled. Jim and I had altered much in our lives to make time for our relationship with Mom. We loved her deeply and enjoyed her immensely. Our grandson Jack had won over everyone in her facility and watching the tenderness between the two of them would melt anyone's heart. But living a care partner's life did create stress and take its toll on our emotions. I altered my retirement plans entirely once mom's dementia required more of me, and truthfully, I was bone-tired and emotionally spent.

There could be no better family members to research and secure a good facility for Mom, and no more compassionate and knowledgeable care partners to manage her current situation all the way through to the inevitable end stage of her dementia. That generous offer would surely have a powerful impact on their lives, too, changing work schedules, retirement plans and the expectation of carefree existence that comes with late middle age.

Yet, rather than feeling immediate gratitude at Lynn and Lowen's offer to take on Mom's caregiving, I was stunned, I was hurt, and to my own surprise, I was angry, thoroughly and completely pissed. *How dare they make that decision without me!*

At the same time, I was conflicted, my intense reaction a surprise to even me. *Who was I to claim the sole right to take care of Mom? Who was I to say no, when Lynn and Peg had every right to want to spend some quality time with her? After all, I had the privilege for many years. Maybe it was their turn.*

Though my heart screamed, "NO, NO!", I did not feel right saying anything but yes. As I struggled to respond, my friend Emily's words haunted me yet again, "She is their mother, too, Kathy. Let them step up and do what they do best. Step back and let them care for her now."

I realized then that, under the anger, the surprise and the pique at not having a say, lurked a deep, heart-stopping grief. I felt like I was losing my mom. It was as if she had died. I had fashioned my life around caring for her. I was not ready for her to go.

Quietly, with patience, in the weeks and successive months following that phone call, my spirit healed of my distress.

Finally, these words formed in my heart, *"Trust Me"*. I felt rather than heard them… *Trust Me.*

I'm Teaching You How to Say Goodbye

So…we sat in the sunshine of an outdoor café on a brilliant Florida fall day, my two new friends from my church and I. One of them had asked me an insightful question, "How are you doing now that your Mom has moved away?"

"I feel like my blessing has been stolen. I wanted to keep it for myself, yet I had to give it up. I wanted to walk Mom all the way home. Now, I may not even be there for her when she goes. She may not even remember me."

My response surprised even me.

Elaine turned to me, and said, "Let me tell you a story. My own grandmother was a wonderful, vital woman, independent and alive with fun and unflinching in her faith. She was my idol, and she cared for me during troubled times in my family. She cared for all of us, really. As my cousins and I grew into adulthood, we all relied on her advice and her strength. But as she grew older, and infirmity slowed first her body, then her mind, she withdrew into herself, communing more and more with her God in prayer, and less and less with us. We worried intensely about her, confronting her one day with this: 'Grandma, what can we do to help you? You seem to be drifting away?' She replied calmly, certain she was fulfilling an important role in this her last season of life, 'I am not going away now, my loves, but I will be soon. Right now, I am teaching you something you need to learn. I am teaching you how to say goodbye.'"

The hair stood up on my arms as she spoke. Over my friend's voice, words echoed in mind, resonating with God's Spirit. "Kathy, I'm teaching you how to say goodbye."

My heart burned with fire. This was His last lesson, one Mom still needed to teach me before her work here with me was done. I was not losing that blessing, it was time for Mom to pass it on.

January 14, 2018

She called last night and said she missed me. She said she had not talked to me in so long and wondered how I was doing. Was Jim well, how about Jackson, Mark, Dave, and the kids?

She rarely remembered how to dial the phone. She was not often clear enough of mind, so this lucid conversation took me completely by surprise. She was totally and wholly there. Wholly aware, in touch and present. We talked of nothing and everything for fifteen to twenty minutes.

Her reaching out to me so moved me it brought tears to my eyes.

The night before her call, I dreamed I had to hurry up to Indiana to see her, to bring Jim and Jack to see her so that we could say goodbye before she died. I remember the rush in my dream to find all my black clothes to pack so that I would be ready for her funeral... and the dream-driven frustration that I could not get plane tickets out that very instant.

I had to get to her. I had to hurry before she left me...before she floated away on a whisper…

"Mommy, my Momma, don't leave me…I miss you so much! I love you, my dear little Momma…I love you."

I let go of her then – trusting her to her Creator, and to my family who now cared for her. I prayed that she would soon find her way home before she lost her capacity to recognize those whom she loved and who loved her back.

My prayer then, stays with me now, as I conclude our story of parallel paths – each taking from the other what God intended, the lessons of a lifetime and the blessings of His Spirit.

As she faded in my mind, I awoke from my dream with these words:

"Go to God, my dear one. Go softly and remember me…for I will carry you with me always…and what you taught me about love, and loss, grace, dignity, and God."

Mom's Path and My Path: Converging as One

As Mom's essence waned, I sensed rather than witnessed her soul's battle, a tug of war between holding on and letting go to birth into another life.

As the grey of her struggle grew darker and darker, her spirit sought the light. It poured over and through me, opening a door to love and grace, bestowing on me a blessing. My own spirit grew lighter and lighter as I learned to relinquish the burden of what only God can carry.

She was still teaching me.

She was teaching me to let go.

She was teaching me to say goodbye.

Epilogue

As I write this, it is the beginning of September 2018, nearly a full 12 months since Mom's move to Indiana.

Over the past year, she settled into life in a beautiful Memory Care facility in Carmel, Indiana, just minutes from Lynn and Lowen and their daughter, Jenny, and family.

They include her in family celebrations, visit her often and indulge her cravings for hot dogs, chocolate milk, and the casseroles from our childhood.

Lynn reports that she has forgotten how to dress herself, but for the most part, she is happy there, though always cold, whether it is 20 degrees outside or 90.

Jim and I visited her three times this year, though distance makes me more clearly understand how Jill, Jay, Lynn, and Peg may have felt when Mom lived here in Florida, far from where they could interact with her on a day-to-day basis.

From time-to-time she gets confused, mixing up the distance from Florida to Indiana, asking me plaintively on the phone, "Why don't you come tomorrow to see me, Kathy? No one comes to see me," forgetting that Peg had driven down from Michigan to visit her for the weekend or that Lynn may have left barely fifteen minutes before.

I talk with her often and flew up again to see her at the end of June, arriving on her 93rd birthday. I brought her a sound machine, the kind that softly soothes with the sounds of rain and tunes one's brain with rolling waves. And, when I left after that weekend, she barely awoke from her drowsy state to say goodbye.

Yet, the dangers that lurk within dementia's delusions are still clearly evident.

On Friday, September 1st, Lynn called from her car on her way to the hospital in Noblesville. Mom had fallen during the night, and the paramedics suspected she broke her hip.

Around 4:00 AM, Mom awoke with a start to see two young men standing in her room. She says she tried to listen to what they were saying but they whispered quietly because they didn't want her to recognize their voices.

More horrifying, she believes that they were trying to pour kerosene on her bed and planned to light it on fire. She hopped up to confront them just as she heard someone yell to them, "Get out of there!"

It was then that Mom felt one of them push her to the floor. "They pushed me right between my shoulder blades, and I went right down. I knew I broke something when I hit the floor."

Filled with adrenaline, she somehow pulled herself up with her walker and hobbled out the hallway, crying for help and raving about the kids in her room who pushed her.

The thing is, there were no male staff members working on her floor that night. The Director of the Unit was in her office already, overseeing the night shift. There are few male residents and those who do live there are confined to wheelchairs.

The boys, the kerosene, the shove in the back – all delusions.

Delusions that carried dire consequences.

Tests during Mom's hospital stay revealed many small blood clots in her lungs and two fractures to her pelvis. The pain medication sedated her enough to drop her oxygen saturation to a dangerous level, so the doctors started her on blood thinners for the clots and oxygen, something never needed before.

Peg drove in that Friday, and I flew in on Saturday to help out, sleeping in rotation with my sisters in Mom's hospital room, in case the delusions arose anew. Jill was able to stop off on her flight from the east coast where she had taken her son to settle into his Junior year at college, staying overnight with us en route to her home in Los Angeles. We called Jay and Stacey, too.

It looked like it would not be long now. Mom was breathing shallowly. The doctors talked of a cascade of complications. We talked of funeral arrangements, and burial plans, of logistics and of our love and admiration for Mom.

Then, she rallied. I swear, Mom is a woman with nine lives!

So, yes, as I write this, Mom is still with us. She transferred to a rehabilitation facility in Noblesville, Indiana on September 4th where she is enduring physical therapy and occupational therapy with dogged determination in the hope that she can walk with her walker again, without blood thinners that make future falls more dangerous, and without supplemental oxygen. Going home on oxygen would mean finding a different residential memory care facility with more skilled nursing care – a move no one wants to impose on her now.

I stayed in Indiana for 12 days, alternating visits to Mom with Lynn and Lowen after Peg and Jill had to return home to work. Each day gave me the opportunity to see first hand the care and attention to medical details that Lynn was able to give Mom. I saw the way her medical expertise made a positive impact on Mom's hospital stay and outcome. I saw how both Lynn and Lowen altered their own retirement plans to be steady caregivers to Mom as her illness enters yet another stage. I experienced myself the hospitality they offered me and my sisters.

This time, too, is ripe with lessons…lessons in trust…a lesson in letting go and stepping back…and a lesson in profound gratitude for my family and the love we all share.

While I write this part of our story, our fierce, little Momma is trying her best to recover. God Bless you, Mom. You are not alone. We all walk this labyrinth together, each trying our best to find our way home.

APPENDIX

A Dementia Care Partner's Manifesto

I choose freely to enter into a care partner relationship with my loved one with the brain disease of dementia. This choice brings with it the responsibility of looking out for her best interests in all cases. I will maintain my loved one's right to determine the course of her life and day to day decisions. I will step in when necessary with guidance and support to sustain that independence for as long as possible.

Should decisions my loved one makes present a danger to her safety or the safety of others, I will have the courage and kindness to step into the gap, redirecting the decision to a more reasonable course of action, regardless of pushback or resistance from my loved one. I will seek the resources, legal authorities, medical and professional advice and the quality of care for my loved one that are needed to provide the best life possible in this the final season.

I will treat my loved one with respect, with dignity, with patience, and with compassion, knowing that my loved one may not always return that treatment in kind. I will remember that her brain disease may cause her to act in ways foreign to her past, and to speak in ways that are not always in keeping with our relationship. I will protect her from others who may not choose to show such respect.

I will take each day as it comes, enjoying the good, the joyful and the endearing as gifts to be savored. As much as possible, I will help fend off her fear, her disorientation, and her volatility by establishing and maintaining a calm routine and proven strategies to divert attention and settle the emotions.

I will communicate frequently, clearly and specifically with others in my family who also care for my loved one, no matter the geographic distance between us. I will seek their input in important decisions, giving time for options to be explored and honoring their wishes where possible without jeopardizing my loved one's wellbeing.

I will care for myself, my family members and my friendships, knowing that burnout is the enemy of a quality care partnership. I will recognize my own need for rest and respite, and for relationship building outside of my care partner role. I will seek balance in my own life and refreshing activities outside of work and my care partnership, so that I may maintain a sense of joy and gratitude for the richness that life brings. I will continue to see my care partner role as a calling, a gift freely accepted, one from which I can learn, grow and become more wholly the person I am meant to be.

Finally, I will honor my loved one as a precious person, a child of God, a sacred soul finding her way home. I will walk with her on this journey as long as I am able, grateful for the parallel paths we walk that allow us to venture together, if only for a time.

Pause to Reflect on Your Own Situation

Pause now to reflect on your own situation with your loved one. Maybe you are facing a similar time in his or her life when confusion and disorganization seem to dominate. Perhaps you have come to the conclusion that your loved one cannot live alone anymore. If so, here are a few things you may want to consider:

When Living Alone Won't Work Anymore

What are the signs that indicate that living alone or in his or her own home may not be the best option?

- Is he or she eating well? Can your loved one still cook, or instead rely on you to provide meals or arrange meals from a service such as Meals on Wheels?
- Have there been falls recently? Even with the furniture and rugs arranged for maximum mobility and safety, has your loved one lost his or her balance and taken a tumble?
- Does your loved one still drive? Is his or her eyesight good enough to navigate at night, or only in daylight hours? Could he or she pass the driver's vision test if required to renew a driver's license?
- If your concern is about your parents, are both still alive and living together? Does one care for the other to the extent that it is wearing on his or her own physical health and well-being?
- Is mail stacking up, bills laying unpaid, and are finances still being looked after appropriately?
- Do you notice confusion or personality changes? Does your loved one express any fear of being alone at night, or of events in the neighborhood, or circumstances in current living arrangements?
- Are you or other family members close enough to physically check in with your loved one regularly to observe his or her living situation?
- Have any of his or her friends or neighbors mentioned

anything to you that may be their way of delivering the message that The Brothers offered to me and Jim?

If any of these rings true, then perhaps it is time to broach the topic of planning for the next life stage with your loved one, before things get to crisis mode. I believe that if we had a plan designed with Mom, rather than imposing a plan on her after each crisis hit, we all may have avoided some of the emotional stress and confusion that ensued at the beginning of her transition out of her own home.

Bottom line: The best time to make plans is when the plans are not yet needed. Talk with your loved ones when the choices are still hypothetical and discussion can pave the way for decisions that ultimately must be made in the future. But even if you find yourself face-to-face with this decision before you have had these discussions, it is never too late to learn about alternatives that are essential to provide the best care while preserving everyone's dignity, safety, and physical and emotional health.

Strategies for Decision-Making

From personal experience, I have learned that there are several things that may help ease the disruption when facing similar decisions:

First, slow down, and I mean slow DOWN. Breathe! Unless, as in our case, there is a true health or safety emergency, this type of major life decision needs time to steep. Allow discussions with everyone involved to simmer for a while if you have the luxury to do so. It IS important to act deliberately and realistically to ensure your loved one's health and safety, but if these issues are not looming large, make such a move only after careful thought and adequate opportunity for lots of input, especially from your loved one, as much as he or she is able.

Take time to talk with your loved one about his or her wishes, long before a move to a new living arrangement is essential. Find out how he or she feels. Does your loved one have strong feelings about staying in their own home? If so, do they have the financial resources in place to provide for support and care as their needs grow, even if dementia sets in? Are there services in their community that offer such home care? If not, what alternatives are most attractive to them? Would they rather live on their own in a supported independent or assisted living arrangement, or move in with one of their kids?

If the latter is what surfaces, are you or any of your siblings ready and able to shoulder the financial, physical and emotional requirements of caring for a loved one in your own home? Are any of these real options based on finances, health, mobility, mental capacity? If not, why not? Which options provide the best potential for quality of life? Finally, what living arrangement would they prefer, and can they afford if they became physically or mentally incapacitated, unable to make their own decisions?

Keep track of discussions in a notebook. These discussions happen best when addressed in small chunks over time. Most people don't enjoy talking about losing their independence so you may have to catch them with snippets of questions or thoughts while sipping a cup of tea during an afternoon visit. You might have to reframe your thinking and language, talking positively to them about preserving as much independence as possible by seeking a more supportive environment. Perhaps pose a discussion about one of their friends who recently made such a decision, then ask what they think.

If you are a parent, do you remember how you learned so much about your teenager's life while driving carpool; you, a fixture ignored in the front seat while they and their friends gossiped? Car rides are great for that – can you get your loved one to share while cruising down the highway on the way to dining out? Once back home, write down options discussed, opinions shared, and any tentative decisions made. Keeping a record of conversations over time will help all parties stay in touch with what really transpired, rather than relying on the emotionally-charged assumptions one can make in times of stress.

Well in advance of a need, research home care, adult day care, independent living, assisted living and memory care facilities in the location where your loved one lives, and in a location closest to the person/s who will ultimately provide oversight to care. Even a year or so early is not too soon to do this exploration, as many facilities have waiting lists. Take your loved one with you when you visit these facilities and help him or her weigh the features and benefits of each. Make a chart if you must, to help you and your loved one keep all options straight. That way, if a situation arises where a move is essential, you will be ready with their first, second and even third choices with a more complete understanding of your loved one's wishes.

Remember, partnering with someone for their care does not necessarily mean moving your loved one or loved ones into your own home, though it may be the right choice for some. In our case, mom always said, "I don't want to live with you kids. I want my own place." Knowing our complicated relationship and her fierce spirit, I was relieved that she felt that way. Her independence was something that I honored and wanted to preserve for her sake and for ours. When thinking of where Mom might move, we looked at lots of alternatives, none of them moving into our spare bedroom.

Be sure to consult with any siblings or other essential family members before launching into any planned move. Even if your siblings or family members live in distant locations, today's technology makes communication simpler if not easier. I encourage you to wade your way through this tough part if your extended family is to survive this caregiving stage intact, still respecting, loving and talking to each other.

This is especially true if your loved one's financial picture requires monetary support from the adult children. Who should contribute what? How will contributions be handled? What about those who take a loved one into their home? How will they be compensated for the time, expense and focus they must provide for your loved one to be safe? How will you divide up the labor, the decisions, the time on deck? Creative solutions abound, just be sure that everyone agrees before placing an expectation on anyone else.

Questions for Your Caring Heart

If you are the soon-to-be caregiver, be sure to weigh your own and your family's lifestyle needs and choices before agreeing to any of the options on the table. It is important to assess your own readiness for a caregiver role and to establish lines of communication with any family members who may be involved in care and decision-making.

Your life matters, too. No one is served if the person who will be providing oversight to care or the care itself is a burned-out mess from stress or their own stress-related illness. Trust me, you don't want to learn this the hard way.

Here are a few questions for your own heart when deciding if you are ready for a caregiving role:

- What has been your relationship with your loved one up until now?
- Are you prepared to put the past behind you and deal with your loved one as he or she is today or will become in the future?
- What emotional and spiritual resources can you draw on as you embark on the caregiver's path?
- Do you have others on whom you can rely? Do you have a friend, partner, or counselor with whom you can discuss your own changes and growth?
- Do you have other family members with whom you need to collaborate?
- What are the signs that you will need to watch for that you are reaching the limits of your own capacity? What changes can you make to streamline demands on you as you begin this caregiving role, and as your loved one's needs grow?
- To whom can you turn to care for your loved one when you are depleted, while you recharge?

When you get down to it, it's all about respect, about honoring one's loved one, honoring one's siblings, honoring one's own family, husband, wife, children, and oneself, so that each person feels heard, each understands the why's and how's of any decision, and each has the opportunity to help shoulder such involvement that will surely increase over time.

If you find that facing this challenge is hurting your own relationships, it is a good idea to seek assistance rather than stumbling through. There are lots of resources out there both online and in many communities to help you sort alternatives and navigate the discussions about senior care. You'll find many of them in the next section of this appendix.

Some Additional Resources for Care Partners

Throughout the course of this journey walking along with mom, I have had to learn an entirely new language and find an entirely new set of tools and resources to help get me and my family through. I am still learning, as is my husband, as are my siblings. Dementia is such an individual disease, but there are some commonalities, strategies for care, and places to learn from each other that I have found over time. I am sure that there are others, but here are just a few of those that I have found most helpful in our situation:

Inspired Living's Dementia Care Series: A support group and educational program for care partners and staff hosted by Inspired Living at Lakewood Ranch, and presented by AJ Cipperly, National Director of Memory Care and Training for Inspired Living. This program uses educational content provided by Positive Approach, used with permission and based on the approach to care created and developed by Positive Approach to Brain Change LLC, Teepa Snow's consulting practice. *(I am sure that some of the Assisted Living and Memory Care facilities in your own town offer support groups. Usually, it is OK to attend, even if you don't yet have a loved one residing in their facility.)*

Positive Approach to Brain Change LLC, Teepa Snow: http://www. teepasnow.com. Ms. Snow is one of the primary thought leaders helping care partners, medical teams and families understand and value the strengths and needs of those living with the brain disease of dementia. Visit this website and take from it what you need, classes, certifications, simply more understanding of what you can do to help your loved one travel this journey with grace and dignity.

Aging Care Newsletter: https://www.agingcare.com. This is a website replete with information, tools, and ideas for establishing a positive care plan for our loved ones. I found the Care Community Questions and Answers from other care partners to be a source of solace, knowledge, and answers that only others also caring for an aging loved one can answer. The perspective offered, and the knowledge I have gained by visiting this site, and subscribing to the email newsletter have been invaluable.

AARP: https://www.aarp.org/caregiving. This enormously rich resource offers guides for every aspect of partnering with another for their care. There is a place to ask questions, and phone numbers to call to get help with specific situations you may be facing. I have learned that AARP has taken on Caregiving as one of its primary focus areas. You can find much that is helpful on this site.

Stephen Ministries: https://www.stephenministries.org/. This is a not-for-profit Christian organization. Stephen Ministry is a lay caregiving ministry that supplements pastoral care. The program teaches laypersons to provide one-on-one care for individuals who request support. The confidential care-giver and care-receiver relationship is usually conducted by weekly visits. Reasons for requesting a Stephen Minister's visits may range from grieving the loss of a loved one, experiencing a major illness or other life difficulties. Check with your pastor or priest to connect with a Stephen Ministry program in your area.

Today's Caregiver Magazine and online resources. https://www.Caregiver.com. This site provides support, resources, newsletters and discussion. Founded in 1995, the organization hosts caregiver conferences, a book club and discussion board for caregivers and professionals in the eldercare field.

National Academy of Elder Law Attorneys: https://www.naela.org/. An organization dedicated to improving the quality of legal services provided to people as they age and to people with special needs.

National Elder Law Foundation: https://www.nelf.org/. The National Elder Law Foundation is the only national organization certifying practitioners of elder and special needs law. They can help you find one of 500 certified elder law attorneys near you.

Veteran's Administration: What is Aid and Attendance? https://www.youtube.com/watch?v=H_tvRSnt_18. This YouTube video gives the criteria for eligibility for this special veteran's pension available to vets and their spouses when one served in a time of war. This pension may assist in financing some of the increasing costs of care as our loved ones age.

Acknowledgements

The journey of writing this book has been a circuitous one filled with starts and stops along the way. Without the partnership with the people listed here, this story may have lived its life only in my own heart. So, to each of these encouraging and honest individuals, I owe my deep gratitude and hearty thanks. To Christa, leader of my first small group for authors, and to Julie who introduced me to the group. Thanks to those members of the group who listened to my initial forays into non-fiction writing, offering their insights and encouragement. Without these other supportive authors, I may not have had the courage to proceed. To D.D. Scott, of LetLoveGlow Author Services my writing coach who taught me to dig deeper and deeper, until I had that first draft completed. Her encouragement, laughter and even tears helped me know I when I was on the right path, and when I needed to try again. Her editing taught me so much about showing, rather than telling the story. To my sisters, Lynn and Peg, who delivered that needed but difficult message, read my manuscript in its roughest form, and graciously encouraged me to keep going to publication. To Jill and her daughter, my niece Flannery, who helped craft the original cover designs. To my fellow authors generously shared their insights and ideas along the way, I thank you.

My gratitude is also due to Kim and her staff at Kim's Angel Care, to Ms. Ellen and Ms. Agnes at DeSoto Beach Club, and Ms. Connie and the staff at Inspired Living. You cared so well and made mom's time there rich and positive. To my friends, Nancy, Mary, Emily, Elizabeth, Richard, Susan, Joanne, Janice, Karin and Elaine, my small group members, and my Andrew Sisters from the Bayside Church Women's Retreat who walked portions of this journey with me and Mom, praying often and listening even more. To our grandson, Jackson, whose understanding of walking in God's light and sharing love with others comes to him so naturally. Thanks for sharing that overflowing love with Great-Grandma. I love you, Jack. Finally, to everyone in the rest of our family, I love you, too. Mark, Terra, Rocco, Natalia, David, Lindsey, JoJo, Lowen, Lynn, Peg, Jay and Stacy, Kaitlyn and Dennis, Megan and Chas, Joe, Dutch, Aaron, Robin, Beau, Drake, Eilee, Sally, Chris, Matthew, Kaelyn, Emilie, Courtney, Doug, Eli, Jenny, Aaron, Logan, Lillian, Ryan,

Jessica, Tammy, Uncle Mike, Aunt Eileen and the rest of the entire extended Milligan crew, I could go on and on …Thanks for loving Mom. Special thanks to Lynn and Lowen who have shouldered her primary care when Jim and I put it down. And most of all, my deepest gratitude to Jim, whose love and continual belief in me over our many years together has been both my anchor and my sail. Your unconditional love and boundless compassion for Mom is worth more than you can ever imagine.

Each of you is precious.
I thank God for sharing you with me.

About the Author

Kathy Flora grew up the second child in a traditional Irish Catholic family of five kids – 4 girls and a boy – with a mom who was trained as an RN at the tail end of WWII, and a dad who gave up a promising professional baseball career when called back into the Marines during the Korean Conflict. Her family moved just about every two years during childhood, finally landing back in the Detroit, MI suburbs where Kathy attended an all girl's Catholic high school, Marian, then on to Michigan State University and Purdue University for her undergraduate and graduate degrees. Later in her career, she attended the Harvard Kennedy School of Government Senior Executive Fellows program.

She is a Nationally Certified Career Counselor and Master Career Coach. She began this work at Purdue University in College Placement. Through successive job changes, she's worked as a consultant, a business executive, organization development and job search trainer, an elected State Representative in New Hampshire, an HR representative at the Congressional Research Service of the Library of Congress, and finally as a leadership program manager in an Intelligence Community agency in the federal service in Washington D. C. and Tampa, Florida.

Kathy's life's passion has been helping others find theirs. She has been a Hospice volunteer, is a leadership and HR blogger for A. J. O'Connor Associates, a volunteer career coach and speaker for CancerandCareers.org, and she delights in spending time helping out at Selah Vie, the local thrift store of Selah Freedom, a national not-for profit organization that fights Human Trafficking on the Suncoast and across the country.

Kathy is a mom, a grandma, a daughter, a sister, a friend and Jim's loving wife, a political junkie, public speaker, novice hiker, and an avid cyclist. She and Jim live in Bradenton, FL, with an inspiring view of the sunsets over the marsh along the Manatee River in a neighborhood with plenty of walking trails and biking paths. Those paths are where she finds her bliss nearly every morning before starting the rest of her day.

This is her first book, and it was a surprise even to her, since she sat down to write on an entirely different topic. But as you may have noticed, God had other plans.

If you have enjoyed this memoir or if it helped you as you walk your own loved one's dementia labyrinth, please drop me an email to tell me your story: kathy@kathyflora.com.

You can also join me on my website and on social media:
Website: https://www.KathyFlora.com
Facebook: https://www.facebook.com/kathy.flora.372
LinkedIn: https://www.linkedin.com/in/kathyflora
Twitter: https://twitter.com/kateatthebeach

Made in the USA
Columbia, SC
05 November 2018